The Poems of Emily Brontë

The Poems of Emily Brontë

edited by Barbara Lloyd-Evans

B.T. BATSFORD LTD · LONDON

Barnes & Noble Books
Savage, Maryland

© Barbara Lloyd-Evans 1992

First published 1992

Typeset by Servis Filmsetting Ltd, Manchester.

and printed in Great Britain
by Mackays of Chatham plc

for the publishers
B.T. Batsford Ltd
4 Fitzhardinge Street
London W1H 0AH

ISBN 0 7134 6590 5

First published in the United States of America 1992 by
BARNES & NOBLE BOOKS
8705 Bollman Place
Savage, Maryland 20763

Library of Congress Cataloging-in-Publication Data

Brontë, Emily, 1818–1848.
    [Poems.   Selections]
    The Poems of Emily Brontë / edited by Barbara Lloyd-Evans.
        p.   cm.
    Includes index.
    ISBN 0-389-20977-5
    I. Lloyd Evans, Barbara.   II. Title.
   PR4172.A4   1992
    821'.8–dc20   91-31921
                                                        CIP

Contents

Introduction

The poems in this book are the poems Emily Brontë herself chose to keep. There are three notebooks extant into which she transcribed her poems – the Ashley manuscript, the manuscript headed 'E.J.B. Transcribed February 1844' (here called the EJB Notebook or EJB MS) and the third, headed 'Emily Jane Brontë Gondal Poems. Transcribed February 1844' (here called the Gondal Notebook or Gon. MS). Of these, the first and third are located in the British Library, the second is missing. There is, however, a facsimile of it in the *Shakespeare Head Brontë*.

There are other poems of hers extant – all on single sheets of paper in various libraries both here and abroad. It seems that a poem was first written on an odd piece of paper, revised and, perhaps, at some later date, copied into a notebook for keeping. As not all poems are included in the notebooks (many on the single leaves of paper are incomplete fragments), some process of selection by Emily was involved.

The first poem of Emily's extant – 'Will the day be bright or cloudy?' – dated 12 July 1836, is on a single leaf, now part of the Bonnell collection in the Brontë Parsonage Library. On one side of this leaf are four poems, of which this is the only one dated. It was not transcribed later into a notebook. On the verso are ten stanzas, or parts of stanzas, that may be separate try-outs for new poems or the early stages in the composition of one long poem. One is dated, June 1838. The fact that paper was used and reused in this economical way must make one wary of poems that are not precisely dated. Their date of composition need not be the same as any one other dated poem near to them. In the notebooks, the earliest poems transcribed are from 1837 (6 March 1837, Gon MS 1).

The last poem of hers extant, an unfinished version of the longer poem that precedes it, is dated 13 May 1848. These two are the last poems entered into the Gondal Notebook and both have many alterations, suggesting that these are not revised transcriptions but early working drafts, written directly into the notebook as she composed them. She entered nothing into the EJB Notebook after 2 January 1846; nothing into the Gondal Notebook after 13 May 1848. More than half the poems in the notebooks (at least nine in the Ashley and all 44 in the Gondal Notebook, a total of 53; the EJB, non-Gondal Notebook has 31 poems) deal with the imaginary world of Gondal, a world that she shared with her sister, Anne.

The Ashley Notebook

This notebook contains the poems Emily chose to transcribe from those she wrote between 26 July 1837 and October 1839 and is unusual in that it is written in longhand. Printed in the Ashley MS section of this collection are numbers 2, 3, 4, 6, 8, 9, 11, 12, 14, 15, 16 of the notebook. Numbers 1, 5, 7, 10, 13 were re-transcribed into the 1844 notebooks and are to be found there.

The EJB Notebook

In February 1844 Emily decided, once again, to transcribe her poems, bringing up to date those she wished to keep. She divided them into two notebooks (see above). The one headed 'Emily Jane Brontë Gondal Poems' is the more flamboyant, with flourishes and lines woven about the words 'Gondal Poems' in the best manner of a well-printed book.

In view of these headings, it seems that there was, for her, a distinction between Gondal and non-Gondal poems (but see Ashley MS Notes p.154). It does not, however, necessarily follow from this that the EJB Notebook is personal in any special confessional, secretive or autobiographical way. The enigma of the relationship of persona to poem in these two notebooks is much the same as that between Shakespeare and his sonnets (EJB Notebook) and Shakespeare and his plays (Gondal Notebook). By separating the poems out, Emily is simply recording that those in the EJB MS do not belong in the Gondal saga and, though they may be revelatory where tone and atmosphere are concerned – these coming, as they do, from the use and reuse of certain words, phrases, images and descriptions – how revelatory, in any specific detail, they are of the private, self-contained person who wrote them must remain speculation.

On the other hand, since there is nothing to suggest that the poems in the EJB MS are early versions to be kept for working over later – indeed some of the best of her poetry is to be found in this notebook – then we surely must accept and honour the difference between the two notebooks, and not, as some have chosen to do, try to fit all her poems into one long-playing Gondal history.

This is further illustrated by the fact that, up to the actual time of the transcribing (from February 1844), the poems are not written up chronologically by date of composition (only two are undated). Neither do they seem to be chosen at random and placed haphazardly, since (up to March 1844) there are certain thematic patterns in both manuscripts. These two facts suggest that both the separation of the two notebooks and the order of their contents (certainly up to about March 1844) was intentional and had a reason.

The relationship of the poems in the EJB MS to Emily's own life and personality is too fraught with guesswork and speculation to have any place in an edition such as this. Her 'mysticism', her 'visions', her possible secret 'love affairs', though perhaps intriguing as a kind of literary gossip, should not affect any valuation that may be made of her poems qua poems.

The Gondal Notebook

As with the poems in its twin manuscript, those in the Gondal Notebook are not entered in chronological order of the dates as given to each poem. Again, in the poems here, up to about March 1844, there seems to be an intended grouping – the first group concerning, for example, a Gondal 'heroine', A.G.A. She is certainly a heroine in modern terms, in that, although a happy child of great promise, she becomes a totally destructive force in Gondal society. Most of the poems are given titles, though many of the later ones are frustratingly enigmatic in their use of initials to refer to Gondal characters. Frequently, one is aware of contemporary influences but more so of the passage of the seasons and the untamed elements of the Yorkshire Moors.

The Gondal Story

The story of the beginnings of the childhood writings of Charlotte, Branwell, Emily and Anne is well documented (by Charlotte and Branwell) and well known. Branwell, in his introduction to the *History of the Young Men Dec. 15th 1830*, writes:

> It was sometime in the summer of the year A.D. 1824 when I, being desirous to possess a box of soldiers, asked papa to buy me one, which shortly afterwards he procured me from Bradford. They were twelve in number, price 1s. 6d., and were the best I ever had. Soon after this I got from Keighley another set of the same number. These soldiers I kept for about a year until either maimed, lost, burnt or destroyed by various casualties they 'departed and left not a wrack behind!'

Branwell carefully logs the various sets he acquires between 1824 and 1828, as a good historian should – he was writing under the name of Captain John Bud at the time, the 'greatest prose writer they [the Young Men] have among them'. He assures us that

> . . . what is contained in this History is a statement of what Myself, Charlotte, Emily and Anne really pretended did happen among the Young Men (that being the name we gave them) during the period of nearly 6 years.

An added note is more personal: 'I first saw them in the morning after they were bought, I carried them to Emily, Charlotte and Anne', where each of them took up a soldier and gave it a name, 'which I consented to, and I gave Charlotte, Twemy [Wellington], Emily, Pare [Parry], to Ann, Trott [Ross],* to take care of them and I to have the disposal of them as I would'.

The 'really pretended' is the hallmark of these early games, as is the assumed position as leader by Branwell himself. They are his soldiers and are merely on loan, to be taken care of in a world of Let's Pretend.

Charlotte's account of the same incident (March 1829) has already a certain romantic novelettish emphasis about it:

> When papa came home it was night and we were in bed, so next morning Branwell came to our door with a box of soldiers. Emily and I jumped out of bed and I snatched up one and exclaimed, 'this is the Duke of Wellington! it shall be mine!' When I said this Emily likewise took one and said it should be hers. When Anne came down she took one also. Mine was the prettiest of the whole and perfect in every part. Emily's was a grave-looking fellow: we called him Gravey. Anne's was a queer little thing very much like herself. He was called Waiting Boy, Branwell chose Buonaparte.

*Parry is Sir W. E. Parry, 1790–1855, Arctic explorer. Ross is Sir John Ross, 1777–1856, Arctic explorer.

Despite the variations in the names bestowed on two of the soldiers (perhaps the older Charlotte had a better memory), the pattern for the 'plays' is established – Branwell and Charlotte on main stage in confrontation, Emily and Anne in the wings, waiting. But what is remarkable is the hold these 'plays' had on their players. Soon the games were well established (1825–c.1828) and began to acquire a literary expression, the first serious one extant being Charlotte's *History of the Year* quoted from above. For Charlotte and Branwell, the spell of Angria (the country that became the centre of the activities of the 'Young Men' and their descendants) held until 1840, when Charlotte was 24 years old, Branwell 23, and the 'real' world encroached on them more harshly than it had done hitherto. In July 1839 Charlotte left home to become a governess and, in December, Branwell a tutor. With Branwell's dismissal from his position in June 1840 and Charlotte's second governess appointment in March 1841, things changed, the centre could not hold and the heyday of the Glasstown Confederacy was over.

For the actors in the wings, much the same pattern must have been followed. One has to say 'must' because concerning their imaginary world of Gondal (a northern island with a climate and flora and fauna akin to those of the Yorkshire Moors) there is nothing extant like the material covering the Glasstown Confederacy. Presumably, they shared the early games but at some time (at least by 1834 when matters Gondalian are mentioned in the 'Diary' for that year) they split off from their dominant elder siblings to create their own focal point for writing. For them, too, this imaginary world had a long-lasting hold. In 1845 Emily and Anne recorded a journey they took, by themselves, to York and Keighley, during which, they 'played at' being various Gondal royal characters escaping from the Palace of Instruction to join their fellow Royalists, who were being hounded by the Republicans. Both Emily, then aged 28, and Anne, aged 25, were still engaged in playing at and writing about Gondal. In their 'Diary' papers of 1845, Emily wrote, 'we intend sticking firm by the rascals as long as they delight us'. Anne is less sanguine, however: 'The Gondals in general are not in first rate playing condition. Will they improve?' One has, of course, to remember that Anne, like Charlotte, was suffering from the 'too much reality' of being a governess. Emily, on the other hand, with the exception of a brief period at Roe Head School as a pupil and a time at Law Hill School as a dogsbody teacher, had remained in the close security of the home, where these dream worlds started and where, with impunity, they could continue.

If the pattern were the same for Emily and Anne, there must have been prose manuscripts about Gondal and its southern, warm, seductive counterpart, Gaaldine. What happened to these manuscripts is not clear. There seem to be two possibilities. The one, that Emily and Anne themselves cleared out their own papers before they died, keeping only poems – no prose pieces (no manuscript of *Wuthering Heights*, for example). Did they keep the poems for possible future publication? Considering the lack of success of the 1846 volume (see below), this seems unlikely. The other possibility, and this seems the likelier, is that when Charlotte sorted out their papers, as she herself records she did, prior to the 1850 edition, she destroyed manuscripts she thought of no use. These would surely have included the Gondal prose pieces, painful mementoes for Charlotte of a passed world and of no immediate interest to a publisher or the reading public. The poems she kept, with (as A.B. Nicholls' transcription tends to indicate) the idea of future publication, cashing in on the fame that the sisters had achieved in their lifetime.

The only prose references (except for a couple of lists of places and people by Anne) to the Gondal saga we have are in the so-called 'Diary' papers that Emily and Anne wrote every four years, recording what they were doing on that day (usually on or near Emily's birthday, 30 July), and were to be opened and read four years later. These 'Diaries' were written in 1834 and 1837, jointly, and 1841 and 1845, separately. In them, the state of play in Gondal is referred to. As many of the references in the poems to Gondal or the Gondal characters are often cryptic, these references in the 'Diaries' might be welcomed as useful in trying to sort out the narrative behind the poems but, on the whole, they offer little help.

It is important to note that when any of the four children wrote about their imaginary worlds, they were not making things up as they went along. The places, the characters and the events were already in existence, were already a part of 'history'. What was written down was not only the chronicles of that history, but commentary on it, stories and poems about its heroes and heroines by either the protagonists themselves or some spying contemporary. So, in the manuscripts of Charlotte and Branwell, although it is Branwell who is the recorder of the chronicles (the historian), he writes, not as Branwell, but as Captain Bud, the greatest prose writer of the (Angrian) time, or as Soult, the equally famous Glasstown poet; although it is Charlotte who fleshes out the chronicles with stories about the characters or writes poems on their behalf, it is not as Charlotte, the novelist, looking in from the outside, but as Charles Townshend, the pseudonym of Lord Charles Albert Florian Wellesley, a member of the Angrian aristocracy (son of the famous Duke of Wellington) and cynical observer of and commentator on matters Angrian.

Undoubtedly, it was in these childhood compositions that Charlotte learnt to write a story wholly convincing as sincere and honest 'autobiography' (*Jane Eyre*) and Emily to write a story untrammelled by conventional morality but narrated, wholly convincingly, as though seen through the eyes of a creature of limited, conventional understanding and even more limited and conventional imagination (*Wuthering Heights*). From her intercourse with the 'real world', Charlotte, when it came to writing for publication, learnt to deal more circumspectly than Emily with the unconventional, amoral web they wove in childhood.

The Gondal poems, then, that we have of Emily's are the embroidery on the basic stuff of Gondal history. From the many manuscripts (both prose and poetry) extant of Charlotte's and Branwell's, we can see something of a coherent picture for the story of the Glasstown Confederacy. For Emily and Anne, having none of their prose manuscripts, we are left in a kind of limbo, with only the embroidery stitching, and no garment underneath.

The History of the Manuscripts

It was in 1845 that Anne wrote in her 'Diary' that Emily was writing the *Emperor Julius's Life*, some of which Emily had read to her, and also poetry, which she had not read to her, for Anne wrote that she 'wonders what it is about?' Emily and Anne had written their 'Diary' papers at the end of July. Did Anne wonder aloud about Emily and her poetry to Charlotte? However Charlotte came to know about the poetry, she showed nothing of the delicate reticence of Anne in her reactions. She wrote in the 'Biographical Notice' to her edition of *Wuthering Heights and Agnes Grey, 1850*:

> One day, in the autumn of 1845, I accidentally lighted on a MS. volume of verse in my sister Emily's handwriting. Of course I was not surprised, knowing she could and did write verse: I looked it over, and something more than surprise seized me – a deep conviction that these were not common effusions, nor at all like the poetry women generally write, I thought them condensed and terse, vigorous and genuine. To my ear they had a peculiar music – wild, melancholy and elevating.

Emily's reaction to Charlotte's prying was one Charlotte never forgot. She had commented earlier in the Notice that, 'formerly we used to show each other what we wrote, but of late years this habit of communication and consultation had been discontinued'. So what Charlotte had done was, as far as Emily was concerned, a kind of treachery. It broke a trust of privacy. As a result:

> My sister Emily was not a person of demonstrative character, nor one on the recesses of whose mind and feelings even those nearest and dearest to her could, with impunity, intrude unlicensed; it took hours to reconcile her to the discovery I had made, and days to persuade her that such poems merited publication. I knew however, that a mind like hers could not be without some latent spark of honourable ambition, and refused to be discouraged in my attempts to fan that spark into a flame . . . We agreed to arrange a small selection of our poems . . .

The 'sub-text' of this description offers a picture of Charlotte hardly suggested elsewhere – interfering, overbearing, ambitious (and ruthless with it), determined, arrogant and stubborn. Emily's subsequent behaviour towards Charlotte, and the elements of guilt that are apparent in Charlotte's own subsequent attitude towards Emily, makes one feel that perhaps true reconciliation never quite happened.

So came about the publication of the *Poems by Currer, Ellis and Acton Bell 1846*, to be followed, after Emily's death in 1848, by the poems Charlotte included in her 1850 edition of the novels, *Wuthering Heights and Agnes Grey*. Her treatment of some of Emily's poems in this volume, even allowing for the passage of time and the increased sensitivity today about altering manuscripts, reinforces the evaluation of some of Charlotte's qualities suggested above. Also, in her changes and additions to Emily's poems, another aspect of Charlotte shows – great novelist though she may have been, she was no poet and, as critic, was not, in the face of the smoothness and propriety thought fitting for poetry at that time, prepared to accept and publish as they stood, with all their 'peculiar music', poems that she had herself recognized as vigorous and genuine.

The 1846 volume contained 21 poems by Emily taken from the two 1844 notebooks (see Appendix) and, of the 1000 copies printed, 961 were sadly still unsold when Smith, Elder and Co. (Charlotte's publishers) purchased the remaining stock in September 1848, a fortnight or so before Branwell's and some three months before Emily's death. The sisters recouped £24 against their initial outlay of about £36.

The 1850 volume contains 18 poems as by Emily (see Appendix 3). Only 17 of these have been traced to a manuscript copy. Whether the eighteenth is a poem of Emily's or is of Charlotte's own composition is debatable. C. W. Hatfield writes: 'The poem seems to express what might well be Charlotte's thought about her sister, but (in the first three verses) not what Emily would write about herself'. I tend to agree with him.

After Charlotte's death, it would seem that the notebooks remained somewhere in the Parsonage, together with the packet, 'about the size of a lady's travelling case', of Charlotte's early writings that Mrs Gaskell read when she was preparing her *Life of Charlotte Brontë* (see the letter of Mrs Gaskell to George Smith, 25 July 1856). In May 1860 poem number 22 of the Gondal MS – 'A Farewell to Alexandria' – was published in the *Cornhill Magazine* under the title of 'The Outcast Mother'.

In 1861, when Mr Brontë died, A. B. Nicholls packed up and returned to Ireland to remarry and settle down. He took with him the family manuscripts. They lay 'in the bottom of a cupboard tied up in newspaper for nearly thirty years' (Clement Shorter, *Charlotte Bronte and Her Circle*, 1896) until, in 1895, Mr Shorter himself, on behalf of T. J. Wise, visited Nicholls in Banagher, and bought the parcel. Their fate at the hands of T. J. Wise was not happy. Manuscripts were wrongly attributed, collected arbitrarily together into morocco-bound private editions, transcribed (often inaccurately) and dispersed, when finished with, in private sales. Odd pages became detached and separated. These loose leaves are now spread across both sides of the Atlantic with, at times, one half of a sheet, say, in Haworth, the other half in some collection in America. Even now the exact location of the EJB Notebook is unknown.

The Ashley MS

2 *To a Wreath of Snow by A.G. Almeda*

'O transient voyager of heaven!
O silent sign of winter skies!
What adverse wind thy sail has driven
To dungeons where a prisoner lies!

'Methinks the hands that shut the sun
So sternly from this mourning brow
Might still their rebel task have done,
And checked a thing so frail as thou

They would have done it had they known
10   The talisman that dwelt in thee,
For all the suns that ever shone
Have never been so kind to me!

For many a week, and many a day,
My heart was weighed with sinking gloom
When morning rose, in mourning grey
And faintly lit my prison room,

But angel-like, when I awoke,
Thy silvery form so soft and fair
Shining through darkness, sweetly spoke
20   Of cloudy skies and mountains bare

The dearest to a mountaineer,
Who, all life long has loved the snow
That crowned her native summits drear,
Better, than greenest plains below –

And voiceless, soulless messenger
Thy presence waked a thrilling tone
That comforts me while thou art here
And will sustain when thou art gone

December, 1837

3 *Song by Julius Angora*

Awake! awake! how loud the stormy morning
Calls up to life the nations resting round,
Arise, Arise, is it the voice of mourning
That breaks our slumber with so wild a sound?

The voice of mourning? Listen to its pealing
That shout of triumph drowns the sigh of woe,
Each tortured heart forgets its wonted feeling,
Each faded cheek resumes its longlost glow –

Our souls are full of gladness, God has given
10   Our arms to victory, our foes to death;
The crimson ensign waves its sheet in heaven –
The sea-green standard lies in dust beneath.

Patriots, no stain is on your country's glory
Soldiers, preserve that glory bright and free
Let Almedore in peace, and battle gory,
Be still a nobler name for victory!

                                December – 1837

4 *Song*

King Julius left the south country
His banners all bravely flying.
His followers went out with Jubilee
But they shall return with sighing

Loud arose the triumphal hymn
The drums were loudly rolling,
Yet you might have heard in distance dim
How a passing bell was tolling

The sword so bright, from battles won
10   With unseen rust is fretting
The evening comes before the noon
The scarce risen sun is setting

While princes hang upon his breath
And nations round are fearing
Close by his side a daggered Death
With sheathless point stands sneering

That death he took a certain aim
For Death is stony-hearted
And in the zenith of his fame
20   Both power and life departed.

April 20th, 1839

6 *Song to A.A.*

This shall be thy lullaby
Rocking on the stormy sea
Though it roar in thunder wild
Sleep   stilly sleep   my dark haired child

When our shuddering boat was crossing
Eldern's lake so rudely tossing
Then 'twas first my nursling smiled
Sleep   softly sleep   my fairbrowed child

Waves above thy cradle break –
10   Foamy tears are on thy cheek
Yet the ocean's self grows mild
When it bears my slumbering child

May 1838

8 *Lines*

I die but when the grave shall press
The heart so long endeared to thee –
When earthy cares no more distress
And earthly joys are nought to me –

Weep not, but think that I have past
Before thee o'er the sea of gloom
Have anchored safe and at last
Where tears and mourning cannot come.

'Tis I should weep to leave thee here
10   On that dark ocean, sailing drear
With storms around and fears before
And no kind light to point the shore

But long or short though life may be
'Tis nothing to eternity
We part below to meet on high
Where blissful ages never die.

December 1837

9 *Song*

O between distress and pleasure
Fond affection cannot be
Wretched hearts in vain would treasure
Friendship's joys when others flee.

Well I know thine eye would never
Smile while mine grieved willingly
Yet I know mine eye forever
Could not weep in sympathy –

Let us part – the time is over
10   When I thought and felt like thee
I will be an ocean rover
I will sail the desert sea

Isles there are beyond its billow
Lands where woe may wander free
And beloved thy midnight pillow
Will be soft unwatched by me.

Not on each returning morrow
When thy heart bounds ardently
Needst thou then dissemble sorrow,
20 Marking my despondency

Day by day some dreary token
Will forsake thy memory
Till at last all old links broken
I shall be a dream to thee.

October 15th. 1839

11

Shed no tears o'er that tomb
For there are Angels weeping
Mourn not him whose doom
Heaven itself is mourning
Look how in sable gloom
The clouds are earthward sweeping
And earth receives them home
Even darker clouds returning

Is it when good men die
10   That sorrow wakes above?
Grieve saints when other spirits fly
To swell their choir of love?

Ah no with louder sound –
The golden harp-strings quiver
When good men gain the happy ground
Where they must dwell forever –

But he who slumbers there
His bark will strive no more
Across the waters of despair
20   To reach that glorious shore.

The time of grace is past
And mercy scorned and tried
Forsakes to utter wrath at last
The soul so steeled by pride

That wrath will never spare
Will never pity know

Will mock its victim's maddened prayer
Will triumph in his woe.

Shut from his Maker's smile
30   The accursed man shall be
Compassion reigns a little while
Revenge eternally.

July 26th 1837

12 *A.A.A.*

Sleep not, dream not this bright day
Will not cannot last for aye
Bliss like thine is bought by years
Dark with torment and with tears

Sweeter far than placid pleasure
Purer higher beyond measure
Yet alas the sooner turning
Into hopeless endless mourning

I love thee boy for all divine
10   All full of God thy features shine
Darling enthusiast holy child.
Too good for this world's warring wild
Too heavenly now but doomed to be
Helllike in heart and misery

And what shall change that angel brow
And quench that spirit's glorious glow
Relentless laws that disallow
True virtue and true joy below
.

And blame me not if when the dread
20   Of suffering clouds thy youthful head
If when by crime and sorrow tossed
Thy wandering bark is wrecked and lost

I too depart I too decline
And make thy path no longer mine
'Tis thus that human minds will turn
All doomed alike to sin and mourn
Yet all with long gaze fixed afar
Adoring Virtue's distant star –

Undated

14 *Lines by Claudia*

I did not sleep 'twas noon of day
I saw the burning sunshine fall.
The long grass bending where I lay
The blue sky brooding over all

I heard the mellow hum of bees
And singing birds and sighing trees
And far away in woody dell
The music of the Sabbath bell

I did not dream remembrance still
Clasped round my heart its fetters chill
But I am sure the soul is free
To leave its clay a little while
Or how in exile misery
Could I have seen my country smile

In English fields my limbs were laid
With English turf beneath my head
My spirit wandered o'er that shore
Where nought but it may wander more

Yet if the soul can thus return
I need not and I will not mourn
And vainly did you drive me far
With leagues of ocean stretched between
My mortal flesh you might debar
But not the eternal fire within

My Monarch died to rule forever
A heart that can forget him never
And dear to me aye doubly dear
Though shut within the silent tomb
His name shall be for whom I bear
This long sustained and hopeless doom

And brighter in the hour of woe
Than in the blaze of victory's pride
That glory shedding star shall glow
For which we fought and bled and died

May 28th, 1839

15 *Lines*

Far away is the land of rest
Thousand miles are stretched between
Many a mountain's stormy crest
Many a desert void of green

Wasted worn is the traveller
Dark his heart and dim his eye
Without hope or comforter
Faltering faint and ready to die

Often he looks to the ruthless sky
10   Often he looks o'er his dreary road
Often he wishes down to lie
And render up life's tiresome load

But yet faint not mournful man
Leagues on leagues are left behind
Since your sunless course began
Then go on to toil resigned

If you still despair control
Hush its whispers in your breast
You shall reach the final goal
20   You shall win the land of rest

October 1837

16 *Lines*

The soft unclouded blue of air
The earth as golden-green and fair
And bright as Eden's used to be
That air and earth have nourished me

Laid on the grass I lapsed away
Sank back again to Childhood's day
All harsh thoughts perished memory mild
Subdued both grief and passion wild.

But did the sunshine even now
₁₀ That bathed his stern and swarthy brow
Oh did it wake I long to know
One whisper one sweet dream in him
One lingering joy that years ago
Had faded – lost in distance dim
That iron man was born like me
And he was once an ardent boy
He must have felt, in infancy
The glory of a summer sky.

Though storms untold his mind have tossed
₂₀ He cannot utterly have lost
Remembrance of his early home
So lost that not a gleam may come

No vision of his mother's face
When she so fondly would set free
Her darling child from her embrace
To roam till eve at liberty

Nor of his haunts nor of the flowers
His tiny hand would grateful bear
Returning from the darkening bowers
₃₀ To weave into her glossy hair.

I saw the light breeze kiss his cheek
His fingers mid the roses twined
I watched to mark one transient streak
Of pensive softness shade his mind

The open window showed around
A glowing park and glorious sky
And thick woods swelling with the sound
Of Nature's mingled harmony

Silent he sat. That stormy breast
40   At length, I said has deigned to rest
At length above the spirit flows
The waveless ocean of repose

Let me draw near 'twill soothe to view
His dark eyes dimmed with holy dew
Remorse even now may wake within,
And half-unchain his soul from sin.

Perhaps this is the destined hour
When Hell shall lose its fatal power
And heaven itself shall bend above
50   To hail the soul redeemed by love

Unmarked I gazed my idle thought
Passed with the ray whose shine it caught
One glance revealed how little care
He felt for all the beauty there

Oh crime can make the heart grow old
Sooner than years of wearing woe
Can turn the warmest bosom cold
As winter wind or polar snow.

April 28th. 1839

The EJB MS

E.J.B.

Transcribed February 1844

1

Loud without the wind was roaring
  Through the waned autumnal sky,
Drenching wet, the cold rain pouring
  Spoke of stormy winters nigh.

  All too like that dreary eve.
  Sighed, within repining grief –
  Sighed at first – but sighed not long
  Sweet. How softly sweet it came!
  Wild words of an ancient song,
  Undefined, without a name –

'It was spring, for the skylark was singing.'
Those words they awakened a spell –
They unlocked a deep fountain whose springing
Nor Absence nor Distance can quell.

In the gloom of a cloudy November
They uttered the music of May –
They kindled the perishing ember
Into fervour that could not decay

Awaken on all my dear moorlands
The wind in its glory and pride!
O call me from valleys and highlands
To walk by the hill river's side!

It swelled with the first snowy weather;
The rocks they are icy and hoar
And darker waves round the long heather
And the fern-leaves are sunny no more

There are no yellow-stars on the mountain
The blue-bells have long died away
From the brink of the moss bedded fountain,
From the side of the wintery brae –

But lovelier than corn-fields all waving
In emerald and scarlet and gold
Are the slopes where the north-wind is raving
And the glens where I wandered of old –

'It was morning, the bright sun was beaming.'
How sweetly that brought back to me

The time when nor labour nor dreaming
Broke the sleep of the happy and free

But blithely we rose as the dusk heaven
40   Was melting to amber and blue
And swift were the wings to our feet given
While we traversed the meadows of dew.

For the moors, for the moors where the short grass
Like velvet beneath us should lie!
For the moors, for the moors where each high pass
Rose sunny against the clear sky!

For the moors, where the linnet was trilling
Its song on the old granite stone –
Where the lark – the wild sky-lark was filling
50   Every breast with delight like its own.

What language can utter the feeling
That rose when, in exile afar,
On the brow of a lonely hill kneeling
I saw the brown heath growing there.

It was scattered and stunted, and told me
That soon even that would be gone
It whispered; 'The grim walls enfold me;
'I have bloomed in my last summer's sun'

But not the loved music whose waking
60   Makes the soul of the Swiss die away
Has a spell more adored and heart-breaking
Than in its half-blighted-bells lay –

The Spirit that bent 'neath its power
How it longed, how it burned to be free!
If I could have wept in that hour
Those tears had been heaven to me –

Well, well the sad minutes are moving
Though loaded with trouble and pain –
And sometime the loved and the loving
70   Shall meet on the mountains again –

November 11th 1838

2

A little while, a little while
The noisy crowd are barred away;
And I can sing and I can smile –
A little while I've holyday!

Where wilt thou go my harassed heart?
Full many a land invites thee now;
And places near, and far apart
Have rest for thee, my weary brow.

There is a spot mid barren hills
10 Where winter howls and driving rain
But if the dreary tempest chills
There is a light that warms again

The house is old, the trees are bare
And moonless bends the misty dome
But what on earth is half so dear –
So longed for as the hearth of home?

The mute bird sitting on the stone,
The dank moss dripping from the wall,
The garden-walk with weeds o'ergrown
20 I love them – how I love them all!

Shall I go there? or shall I seek
Another clime, another sky.
Where tongues familiar music speak
In accents dear to memory?

Yes, as I mused, the naked room,
The flickering firelight died away
And from the midst of cheerless gloom
I passed to bright, unclouded day.

A little and a lone green lane
30 That opened on a common wide
A distant, dreamy, dim blue chain
Of mountains circling every side –

A heaven so clear, an earth so calm,
So sweet, so soft, so hushed an air

And, deepening still the dreamlike charm
Wild moor-sheep feeding everywhere –

That was the scene – I knew it well
I knew the path-ways far and near
That winding o'er each billowy swell
40   Marked out the tracks of wandering deer

Could I have lingered but an hour
It well had paid a week of toil
But truth has banished fancy's power;
I hear my dungeon bars recoil –

Even as I stood with raptured eye
Absorbed in bliss so deep and dear
My hour of rest had fleeted by
And given me back to weary care –

December 4th 1838

3

How still, how happy! those are words
That once would scarce agree together
I loved the plashing of the surge –
The changing heaven the breezy weather

More than smooth seas and cloudless skies
And solemn, soothing, softened airs
That in the forest woke no sighs
And from the green spray shook no tears

10   How still, how happy! now I feel
Where silence dwells is sweeter far
Than laughing mirth's most joyous swell
However pure its raptures are

Come sit down on this sunny stone
'Tis wintery light o'er flowerless moors –
But sit – for we are all alone
And clear expand heaven's breathless shores

I could think in the withered grass
Spring's budding wreaths we might discern
The violet's eye might shyly flash
20   And young leaves shoot among the fern

It is but thought – full many a night
The snow shall clothe those hills afar
And storms shall add a drearier blight
And winds shall wage a wilder war

Before the lark may herald in
Fresh foliage twined with blossoms fair
And summer days again begin
Their glory-haloed crown to wear

Yet my heart loves December's smile
30   As much as July's golden beam
Then let us sit and watch the while
The blue ice curdling on the stream –

December 7th 1838

4

The blue bell is the sweetest flower
That waves in summer air
Its blossoms have the mightiest power
To soothe my spirit's care

There is a spell in purple heath
Too wildly, sadly dear
The violet has a fragrant breath
But fragrance will not cheer

The trees are bare, the sun is cold
10   And seldom, seldom seen.
The heavens have lost their zone of gold
The earth its robe of green

And ice upon the glancing stream
Has cast its sombre shade
And distant hills and valleys seem
In frozen mist arrayed –

The blue bell cannot charm me now
The heath has lost its bloom,
The violets in the glen below
20   They yield no sweet perfume

But though I mourn the heather-bell
'Tis better far away
I know how fast my tears would swell
To see it smile to day

And that wild flower that hides so shy
Beneath the mossy stone
Its balmy scent and dewy eye
'Tis not for them I moan

It is the slight and stately stem
30   The blossom's silvery blue
The buds hid like a sapphire gem
In sheaths of emerald hue

'Tis these that breathe upon my heart
A calm and softening spell
That if it makes the teardrop start
Has power to soothe as well

For these I weep, so long divided
Through winter's dreary day
In longing weep – but most when guided
40 On withered banks to stray

If chilly then the light should fall
Adown the dreary sky
And gild the dank and darkened wall
With transient brilliancy

How do I yearn, how do I pine
For the time of flowers to come
And turn me from that fading shine –
To mourn the fields of home –

December 18th 1838

5

Fair sinks the summer evening now
In softened glory round my home:
The sky upon its holy brow
Wears not a cloud that speaks of gloom –

The old tower, shrined in golden light,
Looks down on the descending sun –
So gently evening blends with night
You scarce can say that day is done –

And this is just the joyous hour
When we were wont to burst away,
To 'scape from labour's tyrant power
And cheerfully go out to play –

Then why is all so sad and lone?
No merry footstep on the stair –
No laugh – no heart-awaking tone
But voiceless silence everywhere.

I've wandered round our garden-ground
And still it seemed at every turn
That I should greet approaching feet
And words upon the breezes borne

In vain – they will not come today
And morning's beam will rise as drear
Then tell me – are they gone for aye
Our sun blinks through the mists of care?

Ah no, reproving Hope doth say
Departed joys 'tis fond to mourn
When every storm that hides their ray
Prepares a more divine return.

August 30th, 1839.

6

Shall Earth no more inspire thee,
Thou lonely dreamer now?
Since passion may not fire thee
Shall Nature cease to bow?

Thy mind is ever moving
In regions dark to thee;
Recall its useless roving –
Come back and dwell with me –

I know my mountain breezes
10   Enchant and soothe thee still.
I know my sunshine pleases
Despite thy wayward will –

When day with evening blending
Sinks from the summer sky,
I've seen thy spirit bending
In fond idolatry –

I've watched thee every hour.
I know my mighty sway –
I know my magic power
20   To drive thy griefs away –

Few hearts to mortals given
On earth so wildly pine
Yet none would ask a Heaven
More like the Earth than thine.

Then let my winds caress thee –
Thy comrade let me be.
Since nought beside can bless thee
Return and dwell with me –

2   May 16th 1841

7

In summer's mellow midnight
A cloudless moon shone through
Our open parlour window
And rosetrees wet with dew –

I sat in silent musing –
The soft wind waved my hair
It told me Heaven was glorious
And sleeping Earth was fair –

I needed not its breathing
10 To bring such thoughts to me
But still it whispered lowly
'How dark the woods will be! –

'The thick leaves in my murmur
'Are rustling like a dream,
'And all their myriad voices
'Instinct with spirit seem.'

I said, 'Go gentle singer,
'Thy wooing voice is kind
'But do not think its music
20 'Has power to reach my mind –

'Play with the scented flower,
'The young tree's supple bough –
'And leave my human feelings
'In their own course to flow'

The Wanderer would not leave me
Its kiss grew warmer still –
'O come,' it sighed so sweetly
'I'll win thee 'gainst thy will –

'Have we not been from childhood friends?
30 'Have I not loved thee long?
'As long as thou hast loved the night
'Whose silence wakes my song?

'And when thy heart is laid at rest
'Beneath the church-yard stone
'I shall have time enough to mourn
'And thou to be alone' –

1   September 11th 1840

8

Riches I hold in light esteem
And Love I laugh to scorn
And lust of Fame was but a dream
That vanished with the morn –

And if I pray – the only prayer
That moves my lips for me
Is – 'Leave the heart that now I bear
'And give me liberty.'

Yes, as my swift days near their goal
10 'Tis all that I implore –
Through life and death, a chainless soul
With courage to endure! –

                    March 1st 1841 –

9

Aye there it is! It wakes tonight
Sweet thoughts that will not die
And feeling's fires flash all as bright
As in the years gone by! –

And I can tell by thine altered cheek
And by thy kindled gaze
And by the words thou scarce dost speak,
How wildly fancy plays –

Yes I could swear that glorious wind
10 Has swept the world aside
Has dashed its memory from thy mind
Like foam-bells from the tide –

And thou art now a spirit pouring
Thy presence into all –
The essence of the Tempest's roaring
And of the Tempest's fall –

A universal influence
From Thine own influence free –
A principle of life intense
20 Lost to mortality –

Thus truly when that breast is cold
Thy prisoned soul shall rise
The dungeon mingle with the mould –
The captive with the skies –

July 6th 1841

10

I'll not weep that thou art going to leave me
There's nothing lovely here,
And doubly will the dark world grieve me
While thy heart suffers there –

I'll not weep – because the summer's glory
Must always end in gloom
And follow out the happiest story,
It closes with the tomb –

And I am weary of the anguish
Increasing winters bear –
I'm sick to see the spirit languish
Through years of dead despair –

So if a tear when thou art dying
Should haply fall from me
It is but that my soul is sighing
To go and rest with thee –

May 4th 1840

11

If grief for grief can touch thee,
If answering woe for woe,
If any ruth can melt thee
Come to me now!

I cannot be more lonely,
More drear I cannot be!
My worn heart throbs so wildly
'Twill break for thee –

And when the world despises –
10   When Heaven repels my prayer
Will not mine angel comfort?
Mine idol hear?

Yes by the tears I've poured,
By all my hours of pain
O I shall surely win thee
Beloved, again!

May 18 1840

12

O Dream, where art thou now?
Long years have past away
Since last, from off thine angel brow
I saw the light decay –

Alas, alas for me
Thou wert so bright and fair,
I could not think thy memory
Would yield me nought but care!

The sun-beam and the storm,
10   The summer-eve divine,
The silent night of solemn calm,
The full moon's cloudless shine

Were once entwined with thee
But now, with weary pain –
Lost vision! 'tis enough for me –
Thou canst not shine again –

November 5th 1838

13

It is too late to call thee now –
I will not nurse that dream again
For every joy that lit my brow
Would bring its after storm of pain –

Besides the mist is half withdrawn,
The barren mountain-side lies bare
And sunshine and awaking morn
Paint no more golden visions there –

Yet ever in my grateful breast
10   Thy darling shade shall (cherished) be
For God alone doth know how blest
My early years have been in thee!

April 1840

14

The wind I hear it sighing
With Autumn's saddest sound,
Withered leaves as thick are lying
As spring-flowers on the ground –

This dark night has won me
To wander far away.
Old feelings gather fast upon me
Like vultures round their prey –

Kind were they once, and cherished,
10 But cold and cheerless now –
I would their lingering shades had perished
When their light left my brow

'Tis like old age pretending
The softness of a child,
My altered hardened spirit bending
To meet their fancies wild

Yet could I with past pleasures,
Past woe's oblivion buy –
That by the death of my dearest treasures
20 My deadliest pains might die

O then another daybreak
Might haply dawn above –
Another summer gild my cheek,
My soul, another love –

October 29th 1839

15

Love is like the wild rose briar,
Friendship, like the holly tree
The holly is dark when the rose briar blooms,
But which will bloom most constantly?

The wild rosebriar is sweet in spring,
Its summer blossoms scent the air
Yet wait till winter comes again
And who will call the wild-briar fair

Then scorn the silly rose-wreath now
10 And deck thee with the holly's sheen
That when December blights thy brow
He still may leave thy garland green –

Undated

16

There should be no despair for you
While nightly stars are burning –
While evening sheds its silent dew
Or sunshine gilds the morning –

There should be no despair – though tears
May flow down like a river –
Are not the best beloved of years
Around your heart forever?

They weep – you weep – It must be so –
10 Winds sigh as you are sighing,
And winter pours its grief in snow
Where autumn's leaves are lying

Yet they revive – and from their fate
Your fate can not be parted
Then man journey onward not elate
But never brokenhearted –

Undated

17

'Well, some may hate and some may scorn
'And some may quite forget thy name
'But my sad heart must ever mourn
'Thy ruined hopes, thy blighted fame' –

'Twas thus I thought an hour ago
Even weeping o'er that wretch's woe –
One word turned back my gushing tears
And lit my altered eye with sneers –

'Then bless the friendly dust' I said –
'That hides thy unlamented head.
'Vain as thou wert, and weak as vain
'The slave of falsehood, pride and pain –
'My heart has nought akin to thine –
'Thy soul is powerless over mine'

But these were thoughts that vanished too
Unwise, unholy, and untrue –
Do I despise the timid deer
Because his limbs are fleet with fear?
Or would I mock the wolf's death-howl
Because his form is gaunt and foul?
Or hear with joy the leveret's cry
Because it cannot bravely die?

No – then above his memory
Let pity's heart as tender be
Say, 'Earth, lie lightly on that breast,
'And kind Heaven, grant that spirit rest!

November 14th 1839

18

Far, far away is mirth withdrawn;
'Tis three long hours before the morn
And I watch lonely, drearily –
So come thou shade commune with me

Deserted one! thy corpse lies cold
And mingled with a foreign mould –
Year after year the grass grows green
Above the dust where thou hast been.

I will not name thy blighted name
10 Tarnished by unforgotten shame
Though not because my bosom torn
Joins the mad world in all its scorn –

Thy phantom face is dark with woe
Tears have left ghastly traces there,
Those ceaseless tears! I wish their flow
Could quench thy wild despair.

They deluge my heart like the rain
On cursed Gommorah's howling plain –
Yet when I hear thy foes deride
20 I must cling closely to thy side –

Our mutual foes – they will not rest
From trampling on thy buried breast –
Glutting their hatred with the doom
They picture thine – beyond the tomb –

But God is not like human kind
Man cannot read the Almighty mind
Vengeance will never torture thee
Nor hunt thy soul eternally.

Then do not in this night of grief
30 This time of overwhelming fear
O do no think that God can leave
Forget, forsake, refuse to hear! –

What have I dreamt? He lies asleep
With whom my heart would vainly weep
He rests – and I endure the woe
That left his spirit long ago –

March 1840

19

I see around me piteous tombstones grey
Stretching their shadows far away.
Beneath the turf my footsteps tread
Lie low and lone the silent dead –
Beneath the turf, beneath the mould –
Forever dark, forever cold –
And my eyes cannot hold the tears
That memory hoards from vanished years
For Time and Death and Mortal pain
10 Give wounds that will not heal again –
Let me remember half the woe
I've seen and heard and felt below
And Heaven itself, so pure and blest
Could never give my spirit rest –
Sweet land of light! thy children fair
Know nought akin to our despair, –
Nor have they felt, nor can they tell
What tenants haunt each mortal cell
What gloomy guests we hold within –
20 Torments and madness, tears and sin!
Well – may they live in ecstasy
Their long eternity of joy;
At least we would not bring them down
With us to weep, with us to groan,
No – Earth would wish no other sphere
To taste her cup of sufferings drear;
She turns from Heaven a careless eye
And only mourns that _we_ must die!
Ah mother, what shall comfort thee
30 In all this (mindless) misery?
To cheer our eager eyes a while
We see thee smile, how fondly smile!
But who reads not through that tender glow
Thy deep, unutterable woe?
Indeed no dazzling land above
Can cheat thee of thy children's love –
We all in life's departing shine
Our last dear longings blend with thine;
And struggle still, and strive to trace
40 With clouded gaze thy darling face
We would not leave our native home
For _any_ world beyond the tomb
No – rather on thy kindly breast
Let us be laid in lasting rest
Or waken but to share with thee
A mutual immortality –

20

The evening passes fast away,
'Tis almost time to rest –
What thoughts has left the vanished day?
What feelings in thy breast?

'The vanished day? it leaves a sense
'Of labour hardly done –
'Of little gained with vast expense –
'– A sense of grief alone –'

'Time stands before the door of Death
10   'Upbraiding bitterly
'And conscience, with exhaustless breath
'Pours black reproach on me –

'And though I think that Conscience lies
'And Time should Fate condemn –
'Still, weak Repentance clouds my eyes,
'And makes me yield to them'

Then art thou glad to seek repose?
– Art glad to leave the sea?
And anchor all thy weary woes
20   In calm Eternity?

Nothing regrets to see thee go –
Not one voice sobs, 'Farewell'
And where thy heart has suffered so
Canst thou desire to dwell?

'Alas! the countless links are strong
'That bind us to our clay;
'The loving spirit lingers long
'And would not pass away –

'And rest is sweet, when laurelled fame
30   'Will crown the soldier's crest;
'But a brave heart with a tarnished name
'Would rather fight, than rest,'

Well thou hast fought for many a year
– Hast fought thy whole life through.
– Hast humbled Falsehood – trampled Fear.
What is there left to do?

'"Tis true – this arm has hotly striven,
'Has dared what few would dare
'Much have I done, and freely given –
40   'Yet little learnt to bear' –

Look on the grave where thou must sleep
Thy last and strongest foe –
'Twill be endurance not to weep
If that repose be woe

The long fight closing in defeat.
Defeat serenely borne –
Thine eventide may still be sweet –
Thy night, a glorious morn –

            October 23rd – 42 – February 6th 1843

21 *Hope*

Hope was but a timid Friend –
She sat without the grated den
Watching how my fate would tend,
Even as selfish-hearted men –

She was cruel in her fear.
Through the bars, one dreary day,
I looked out to see her there
And she turned her face away!

Like a false guard, false watch keeping
10   Still in strife, she whispered, peace
She would sing while I was weeping,
If I listened, she would cease –

False she was, and unrelenting.
When my last joys strewed the ground
Even sorrow saw repenting
Those sad relics scattered round –

Hope – whose whisper would have given –
Balm to all that frenzied pain –
Stretched her wings and soared to heaven –
20   Went – and ne'er returned again!

            December 18th 184–

22 *My Comforter*

Well has thou spoken – and yet not taught
A feeling strange or new –
Thou hast but roused a latent thought,
A cloud-closed beam of sunshine brought
To gleam in open view –

Deep down – concealed within my soul
That light lies hid from men
Yet glows unquenched – though shadows roll,
Its gentle ray can not control,
10   – About the sullen den –

Was I not vexed, in these gloomy ways
To walk unlit so long?
Around me, wretches uttering praise
Or howling o'er their hopeless days –
And each with frenzy's tongue –

A Brotherhood of misery,
With smiles as sad as sighs –
Whose madness daily maddening me,
Turning into agony
20   The Bliss before my eyes –

So stood I – in Heaven's glorious sun
And, in the glare of Hell
My spirit drank a mingled tone
Of seraph's song and demon's groan.
– What thy soul bore thy soul alone
Within its self may tell –

Like a soft air above a sea
Tossed by the tempest's stir –
A thawwind melting quietly
30   The snowdrift on some wintery lea
– No – What sweet thing can match with thee,
My thoughtful Comforter?

And yet a little longer speak
Calm this resentful mood
And while the savage heart grows meek,
For other token do not seek,
But let the tear upon my cheek
40   Evince my gratitude –

                                February 10th 1844

23

How clear she shines! How quietly
I lie beneath her silver light
While Heaven and Earth are whispering me,
'Tomorrow wake – but dream tonight' –

Yes – Fancy come, my faery love!
These throbbing temples, softly kiss.
And bend my lonely couch above
And bring me rest, and bring me bliss –

The world is going. Dark world adieu!
10 Grim world, go hide thee till the day;
The heart thou canst not all subdue
Must still resist if thou delay.

Thy love, I will not – will not share
Thy hatred only wakes a smile
Thy griefs may wound – thy wrongs may tear
But oh thy lies shall ne'er beguile –

While gazing on the stars that glow
Above me in that stormless sea
I long to Hope that all the woe
20 Creation knows, is held in thee! –

And this shall be my dream tonight –
I'll think the heaven of glorious spheres
Is rolling on its course of light
In endless bliss, through endless years –

I'll think, there's not one world above,
Far as these straining eyes can see,
Where Wisdom ever laughed at Love –
Or Virtue crouched to Infamy –

Where – writhing neath the strokes of Fate
30 The mangled wretch is forced to smile,
To match his patience 'gainst his hate,
His heart rebellious all the while.

Where Pleasure still will lead to wrong
And helpless Reason warn in vain
And Truth is weak, and Treachery strong
And Joy the shortest path to pain –

And Peace the lethargy of grief –
And Hope a phantom of the Soul –
And Life a labour void and brief –
40   And Death the despot of the whole –

April 13th 1843 –

24

On a sunny brae alone I lay
One summer afternoon,
It was the marriage-time of May
With her young lover, June.

From her Mother's heart seemed loath to part
That queen of bridal charms;
But her Father smiled on the fairest child
He ever held in his arms

The trees did wave their plumy crests,
10   The glad birds carolled clear
And I, of all the wedding guests
Was only sullen there –

There was not one but wished to shun
My aspect void of cheer
The very grey rocks looking on
Asked, 'what do you do here?'

And I could utter no reply –
In sooth I did not know
Why I had brought a clouded eye
20   To greet the general glow,

So resting on a heathy bank
I took my heart to me
And we together sadly sank
Into a reverie

We thought – 'When winter comes again
Where will these bright things be?
All vanished like a vision vain –
An unreal mockery!

The birds that now so blithely sing –
30 Through deserts frozen dry,
Poor spectres of the perished Spring
In famished troops will fly

And why should we be glad at all?
The leaf is hardly green
Before a token of the fall
Is on its surface seen –'

Now whether it were really so
I never could be sure –
But as in fit of peevish woe
40 I stretched me on the moor

A thousand thousand glancing fires
Seemed kindling in the air –
A thousand thousand silvery lyres
Resounded far and near

Methought the very breath I breathed
Was full of sparks divine
And all my heather couch was wreathed
By that celestial shine –

And while the wide Earth echoing rang
50 To their strange minstrelsy
The little glittering spirits sang
Or seemed to sing to me –

'O mortal, mortal, let them die –
'Let Time and Tears destroy
'That we may over–flow the sky
'With universal joy –

'Let Grief distract the sufferer's breast
'And Night obscure his way
'They hasten him to endless rest
60 'And everlasting day

'To Thee the world is like a tomb.
'A desert's naked shore
'To us – in unimagined bloom
'It brightens more and more.

'And could we lift the veil and give
'One brief glimpse to thine eye
'Thou would'st rejoice for those that live
'Because they live to die –'

The music ceased – the noon day Dream
70 Like dream of night withdrew
But Fancy still will sometimes deem
Her fond creation true –

March 5th 1844

25 *To Imagination*

When weary with the long day's care
And earthly change from pain to pain
And lost and ready to despair
Thy kind voice calls me back again –
O my true Friend, I am not lone
While thou canst speak with such a tone!

So hopeless is the world without
The world within I doubly prize
Thy world, where guile and hate and doubt
10 And cold suspicion never rise –
Where thou and I and Liberty
Have undisputed sovereignty.

What matters it that all around
Danger and grief and darkness lie
If but within our bosom's bound
We hold a bright unsullied sky
Warm with the thousand mingled rays
Of suns that know no winter days –

Reason indeed may oft complain
20 For Nature's sad reality
And tells the suffering heart how vain
Its cherished dreams must always be
And Truth may rudely trample down
The flowers of fancy newly blown

But thou art ever there to bring
The hovering visions back and breathe
New glories o'er the blighted spring
And call a lovelier life from death
And whisper with a voice divine
Of real worlds as bright as thine

I trust not to thy phantom bliss
Yet still in evening's quiet hour
With never failing thankfulness
I welcome thee benignant power
Sure Solacer of human cares
And brighter hope when hope despairs –

September 3rd 1844

26

O! thy bright eyes must answer now,
When Reason, with a scornful brow,
Is mocking at my overthrow;
O, thy sweet tongue must plead for me
And tell why I have chosen thee!

Stern Reason is to judgement come
Arrayed in all her forms of gloom;
Wilt thou my advocate he dumb?
No radiant angel, speak and say
Why I did cast the world away:

Why I have persevered to shun
The common paths that others run
And on a strange road journeyed on,
Heedless alike of Wealth and Power –
Of Glory's wreath and Pleasure's flower –

These once indeed seemed Beings divine
And they perchance heard vows of mine
And saw my offerings on their shrine –
But, careless gifts are seldom prized
And mine were worthily despised;

So with a ready heart I swore
To seek their altar stone no more
And gave my spirit to adore

Thee, ever present, phantom thing.
My slave, my Comrade and my King!

A slave because I rule thee still
Incline thee to my changeful will
And make thy influence good or ill –
A comrade, for by day and night
30 Thou art my intimate Delight –

My Darling Pain that wounds and sears
And wrings a blessing out from tears
By deadening me to real cares:
And yet a king – though prudence well
Have taught thy subject to rebel –

And am I wrong, to worship where
Faith cannot doubt, nor Hope despair,
Since my own soul can grant my prayer?
Speak God of visions, plead for me,
40 And tell why I have chosen thee!

October 14th 1844

27

'Enough of Thought, Philosopher,
'Too long hast thou been dreaming
'Unlightened, in this chamber drear
'While summer's sun is beaming –
'Space-sweeping soul, what sad refrain
'Concludes thy musings once again?

'O for the time when I shall sleep
'Without identity –
'And never care how rain may steep
10 'Or snow may cover me!

'No promised Heaven, these wild Desires
'Could all or half fufil –
'No threatened Hell – with quenchless fires
'Subdue this quenchless will!'

– So said I . . and still say the same, –
– Still to my Death will say –
Three Gods within this little frame
Are warring night and day –

Heaven could not hold them all, and yet
20 They all are held in me
And must be mine till I forget
My present entity –

O, for the time, when in my breast
Their struggles will be o'er.
O for the day when I shall rest
And never suffer more!

'I saw a spirit standing, Man,
'Where thou doest stand – an hour ago,
'And round his feet, three rivers ran
30 'Of equal depth and equal flow –

'A Golden stream, and one like blood
'And one like Sapphire, seemed to be
'But where they joined their triple flood
'It tumbled in an inky sea –

'The Spirit bent his dazzling gaze
'Down on that ocean's gloomy night
'Then – kindling all with sudden blaze
'The glad deep sparkled wide and bright

'White as the sun far, far more fair
40   'Than its divided sources were!'

– And even for that spirit, Seer,
I've watched and sought my lifetime long
Sought Him in Heaven, Hell, Earth and Air
An endless search – and always wrong!

Had I but seen his glorious eye
Once light the clouds that wilder me,
I ne'er had raised this coward cry
To cease to think and cease to be –

I ne'er had called oblivion blest
50   Nor stretching eager hands to Death
Implored to change for lifeless rest
This sentient soul this living breath

O let me die that power and will
Their cruel strife may close
And vanquished Good victorious Ill
Be lost in one repose

February 3d 1845.

(Opposite) *Map of Angria created and drawn by Branwell*

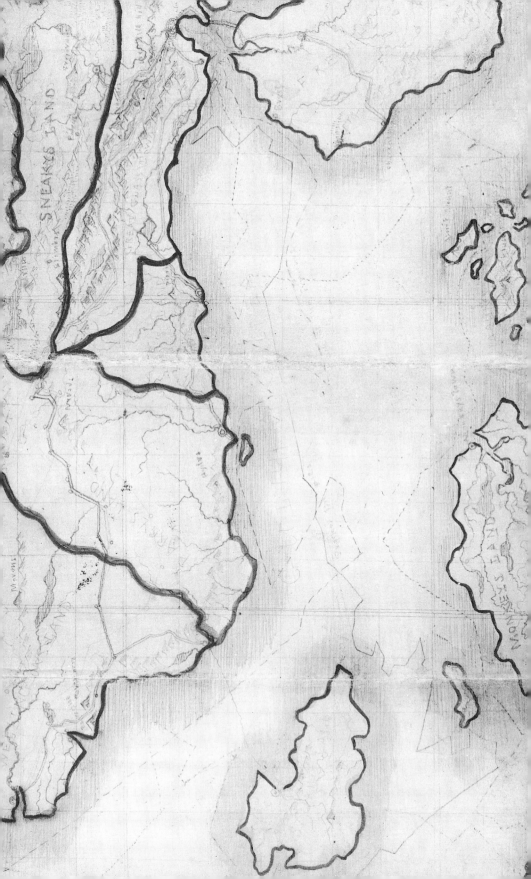

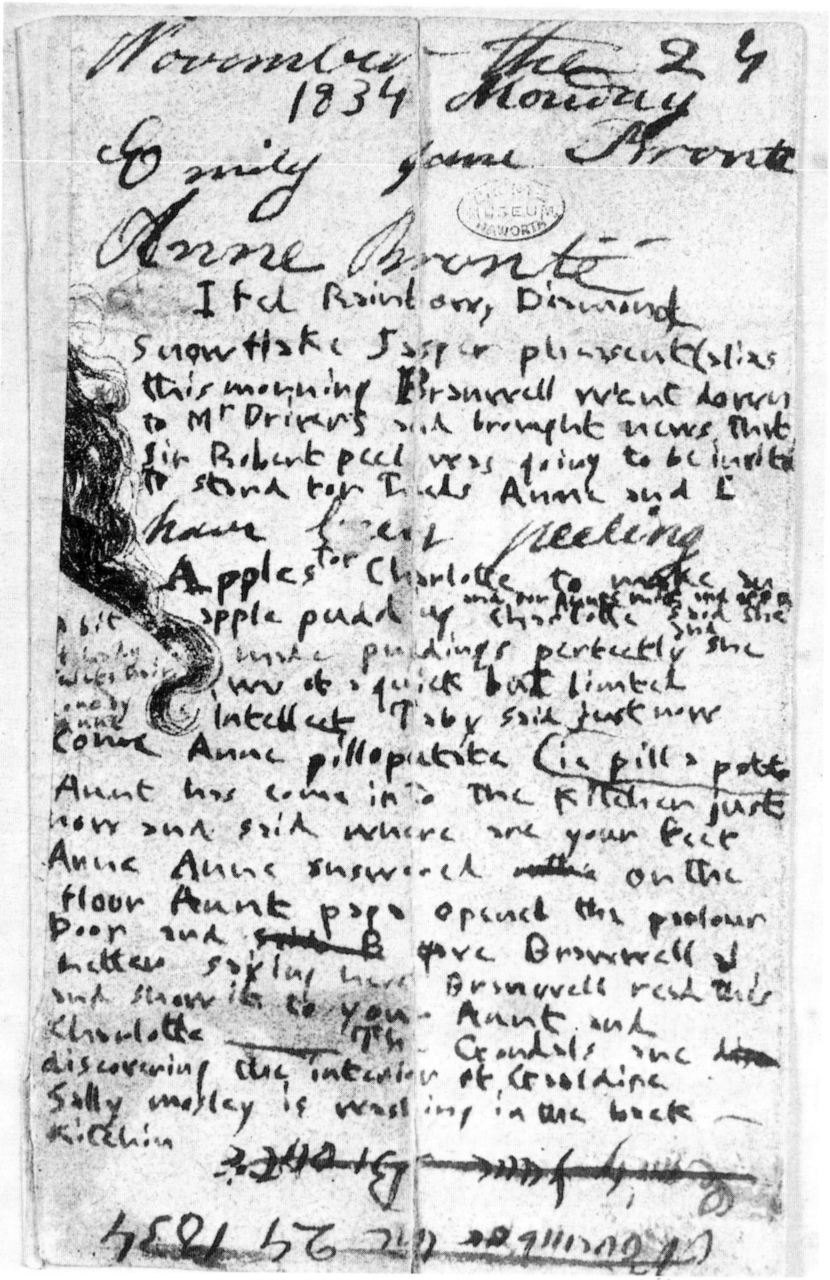
November the 24 1834 Monday
Emily Jane Bronte
Anne Bronte
I fed Rainbow, Diamond Snowflake Jasper pheasent (alias this morning Branwell went down to Mr Drivers and brought news that Sir Robert peel was going to be invited to stand for Leeds Anne and I have been peeling Apples for Charlotte to make an apple pudding and for Aunts nuts and apple Charlotte said she [illegible] puddings perfectly she was of a quick but limited intellect Taby said just now Come Anne pillopatate (ie pill a potate) Aunt has come into the Kitchen just now and said where are your feet Anne Anne answered On the floor Aunt papa opened the parlour Door and gave Branwell a Letter saying here Branwell read this and show it to your Aunt and Charlotte The Gondals are discovering the interior of Gaaldine Sally mosley is washing in the back Kitchen
a bit of Lady Victoria's hair done by Anne
November the 24 1834

Emily and Anne' 'diary paper' of 24 November 1834

Emily's 'diary paper' of 26 June 1837, with her drawing of
herself and Anne at the table, writing

Part of Emily's 'diary paper' of 31 July 1845 with her drawing of her bedroom, herself and her dog, Keeper

Pages from the Ashley MS (the last 4 stanzas of no. 11 and the first 3 of no. 12), written in longhand (see pages 21 to 22).

Emily Jane Brontë.   Transcribed February 1844

Gondal Poems

A.G.A.   March 6th 1837

There shines the moon, at noon of night,
Vision of Glory—Dream of light!
Holy as heaven—undimmed and pure,
Looking down on the lonely moor—
And lonelier still beneath her ray
That drear moor stretches far away

Till it seems strange that aught can lie
Beyond its zone of silver sky—

Bright moon—dear moon! when years have past
My weary feet return at last—
And still upon Lake Elnor's breast
Thy solemn rays serenely rest
And still are Fir-trees sighing move
Like mourners over Elbë's grove
And Earth's the same but Oh to see
How wildly Time has altered me!
Am I the being who long ago
Sat watching by that water side
The light of life expiring slow
From his fair cheek and brow of pride?
Not oft these mountains feel the shine
Of such a day—as fading then,
Cast from its bank of clouds divine
A last smile o'er the heathery plain
And kissed the far-off peaks of snow
That gleaming on the horizon shine
As if in summer's warmest glow
Stern winter claimed a sable shrine—
And there he lay among the bloom
His rich blood dyed a deeper hue
Shuddering to feel the ghastly gloom
That coming Death around him threw—

No Coward Soul Is Mine – *the last poem, dated 2 January 1846, in the E.J.B. MS (see page 71).*

(Opposite) The first page of the Gondal MS (see page 75).

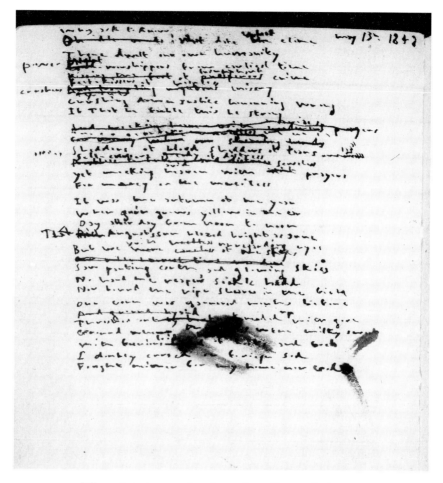

Why ask to know what date what clime – *the last poem,
dated 13 May 1848, in the Gondal MS: incomplete and difficult
to decipher (see page 147).*

28

Ah! why, because the dazzling sun
Restored my earth to joy
Have you departed, everyone,
And left a desert sky?

All through the night, your glorious eyes
Were gazing down in mine
And with a full heart's thankful sighs
I blessed that watch divine!

I was at peace: and drank your beams
10   As they were life to me
And revelled in my changeful dreams
Like petrel on the sea –

Thought followed thought – star followed star
Through boundless regions on
While one sweet influence, near and far,
Thrilled through and proved us one.

Why did the morning rise to break
So great, so pure a spell,
And scorch with fire the tranquil cheek
20   Where your cool radiance fell?

Blood red he rose, and arrow-straight
His fierce beams struck my brow
The soul of Nature sprang elate,
But mine sank sad and low!

My lids closed down – yet through their veil
I saw him blazing still;
And bathe in gold the misty dale
And flash upon the hill –

I turned me to the pillow then
30   To call back Night, and see
Your worlds of solemn light again
Throb with my heart and me!

It would not do – the pillow glowed
And glowed both roof and floor
And birds sang loudly in the wood
And fresh winds shook the door.

The curtains waved, the wakened flies
Were murmuring round my room
Imprisoned there, till I should rise
40   And give them leave to roam –

O, Stars and Dreams and Gentle Night.
O, Night and Stars return!
And hide me from this hostile light
That does not warm, but burn –

That drains the blood of suffering men –
Drinks tears, instead of dew –
Let me sleep through his blinding reign
And only wake with you!

April 14th 1845

29

Death, that struck when I was most confiding
In my certain Faith of joy to be;
Strike again, Time's withered branch dividing
From the fresh root of Eternity!

Leaves, upon Time's branch, were growing brightly
Full of sap and full of silver dew;
Birds, beneath its shelter, gathered nightly;
Daily, round its flowers, the wild bees flew.

Sorrow passed and plucked the golden blossom,
10   Guilt stripped off the foliage in its pride;
But, within its parents kindly bosom
Flowed forever Life's restoring tide –

Little mourned I for the parted gladness,
For the vacant nest and silent song;
Hope was there and laughed me out of sadness,
Whispering, 'Winter will not linger long'.

And behold, with tenfold increase blessing
Spring adorned the beauty-burdened spray;
Wind and rain and fervent heat caressing
20   Lavished glory on its second May –

High it rose, no winged grief could sweep it,
Sin was scared to distance with its shine:

Love and its own life had power to keep it
From all wrong, from every blight but thine! –

Death, the young leaves droop and languish!
Evening's gentle air may still restore –
No, the morning sunshine mocks my anguish –
Time for me must never blossom more –

Strike it down – that other boughs may flourish
30 Where that perished sapling used to be;
Thus, at least, its mouldering corpse will nourish
That from which it sprung, Eternity –

April 10th 1845

30

How beautiful the Earth is still
To thee, how full of Happiness;
How little fraught with real ill
Or shadowy phantoms of distress:

How spring can bring thee glory yet,
And summer win thee to forget
December's sullen time!
Why dost thou hold the treasure fast
Of youth's delight, when youth is past
10 And thou art near thy prime?

When those who were thy own compeers
Equal in fortunes and in years
Have seen their morning melt in tears
To dull unlovely day;
Blest, had they died unproved and young
Before their hearts were wildly wrung
Poor slaves, subdued by passions strong
A weak and helpless prey!

'Because, I hoped while they enjoyed
20 'And by fulfilment, hope destroyed –
'As children hope, with trustful breast
'I waited Bliss and cherished Rest –

'A thoughtful Spirit taught me soon
'That we must long till life be done
'That every phase of earthly joy
'Will always fade and always cloy –

'This I foresaw, and would not chase
'The fleeting treacheries
'But with firm foot and tranquil face
30   'Hold backward from that tempting race;
'Gazed o'er the sands, the waves efface
'To the enduring seas –

'There cast my anchor of Desire
'Deep in unknown Eternity
'Nor ever let my spirit tire
'With looking for <u>What is to Be</u>.

'It is Hope's spell that glorifies
'Like youth to my maturer eyes
'All Nature's million mysteries –
40   'The fearful and the fair –

'Hope soothes me in the griefs I know
'She lulls my pain for other's woe
'And makes me strong to undergo
'What I am born to bear.

'Glad comforter, will I not brave
'Unawed, the darkness of the grave.
'Nay, smile, to hear Death's billows rave
'My guide, sustained by thee?
'The more unjust seems present Fate
50   'The more my spirit springs elate
'Strong in thy strength to anticipate
'Rewarding Destiny!'

June 2d 1845 –

31

No coward soul is mine
No trembler in the world's storm-troubled sphere.
I see Heaven's glories shine
And Faith shines equal arming me from Fear

O God within my breast
Almighty ever-present Deity
Life, that in me hast rest
As I Undying Life, have power in thee

Vain are the thousand creeds
10 That move men's hearts, unutterably vain,
Worthless as withered weeds
Or idlest froth amid the boundless main

To waken doubt in one
Holding so fast by thy infinity
So surely anchored on
The steadfast rock of Immortality

With wide-embracing love
Thy spirit animates eternal years
Pervades and broods above,
20 Changes, sustains, dissolves, creates and rears

Though Earth and moon were gone
And suns and universe ceased to be
And thou wert left alone
Every Existence would exist in thee

There is not room for Death
Nor atom that his might could render void
Since Thou art Being and Breath
And what thou art may never be destroyed

Jan 2nd 1846

The Gondal MS

Emily Jane Brontë

Transcribed February 1844

GONDAL POEMS

1 *A.G.A.*

There shines the moon, at noon of night.
Vision of Glory – Dream of light!
Holy as heaven – undimmed and pure,
Looking down on the lonely moor –
And lonelier still beneath her ray
That drear moor stretches far away
Till it seems strange that aught can lie
Beyond its zone of silver sky –

Bright moon – dear moon! when years have past
10 My weary feet return at last –
And still upon Lake Elnor's breast
Thy solemn rays serenely rest
And still the fern-leaves sighing wave
Like mourners – over Elbë's grave
And Earth's the same but Oh to see
How wildly Time has altered me!
Am I the being who long ago
Sat watching by that water side
The light of life expiring slow
20 From his fair cheek and brow of pride?
Not oft these mountains feel the shine
Of such a day – as fading then,
Cast from its fount of gold divine
A last smile on the heathery plain
And kissed the far-off peaks of snow
That gleaming on the horizon shone
As if in summer's warmest glow
Stern winter claimed a loftier throne –
And there he lay among the bloom
30 His red blood dyed a deeper hue
Shuddering to feel the ghostly gloom
That coming Death around him threw –
Sickening to think one hour would sever
The sweet, sweet world and him for ever
To think that twilight gathering dim
Would never pass away to him –
No – never more! That awful thought
A thousand dreary feelings brought
And memory all her powers combined
40 And rushed upon his fainting mind.

Wide, swelling woodlands seemed to rise
Beneath soft, sunny, southern skies –

Old Elbë Hall his noble home
Tower'd mid its trees, whose foliage green
Rustled with the kind airs that come
From summer Heavens when most serene –
And bursting through the leafy shade
A gush of golden sunlight played;
Bathing the walls in amber light
50   And sparkling in the water clear
That stretched below – reflected bright
The whole, wide world of cloudless air –
And still before his spirit's eye
Such wellknown scenes would rise and fly
Till, maddening with despair and pain
He turned his dying face to me
And wildly cried, 'Oh once again
'Might I my native country see!
'But once again – one single day!
60   'And must it – can it <u>never</u> be?
'To die – and die so far away
'When life has hardly smiled for me –
'Augusta – you will soon return
'Back to that land in health and bloom
'And then the heath alone will mourn
'Above my unremembered tomb,
'For you'll forget the lonely grave
'And mouldering corpse by Elnor's wave' –

*   *   *

March 6th 1837

2 *A.G.A. to A.E.*

Lord of Elbë, on Elbë hill
The mist is thick and the wind is chill
And the heart of thy Friend from the dawn of day
Has sighed for sorrow that thou went away –

Lord of Elbë, how pleasant to me
The sound of thy blithesome step would be
Rustling the heath that, only now
Waves as the night-gusts over it blow

Bright are the fires in thy lonely home
10   I see them far off, and as deepens the gloom
Gleaming like stars through the high forest-boughs
Gladder they glow in the park's repose –

O Alexander! when I return,
Warm as those hearths my heart would burn,
Light as thine own, my foot would fall
If I might hear thy voice in the hall –

But thou art now on a desolate sea –
Parted from Gondal and parted from me –
All my repining is hopeless and vain,
20   Death never yields back his victims again –

August 19th 1837

3 *A.G.A. to A.S.*

At such a time, in such a spot
The world seems made of light
Our blissful hearts remember not
How surely follows night –

I cannot, Alfred, dream of aught
That casts a shade of woe:
That heaven is reigning in my thought
Which wood and wave and earth have caught
From skies that overflow –

10   That heaven which my sweet lover's brow
Has won me to adore –
Which from his blue eyes beaming now
Reflects a still intenser glow
Than nature's heaven can pour –

I know our souls are all divine
I know that when we die
What seems the vilest, even like thine
A part of God himself shall shine
In perfect purity –

20 But coldly breaks November's day;
Its changes charmless all
Unmarked, unloved, they pass away
We do not wish one hour to stay
Nor sigh at evening's fall

And glorious is the gladsome rise
Of June's rejoicing morn
And who, with unregretful eyes
Can watch the lustre leave its skies
To twilight's shade forlorn?

30 Then art thou not my golden June,
All mist and tempest-free?
As shines earth's sun in summer noon
So heaven's sun shines in thee –

Let others seek its beams divine
In cell and cloister drear
But I have found a fairer shrine
A happier worship here –

By dismal rites they win their bliss
By penance, fasts, and fears –
40 I have one rite – a gentle kiss –
One penance – tender tears –

O could it thus forever be
That I might so adore
I'd ask for all eternity,
To make a paradise for me,
My love – and nothing more!

May 6th 1840
July 28th 1843

4 *To A.G.A.*

'Thou standest in the green-wood now
'The place, the hour, the same –
'And here the fresh leaves gleam and glow
'And there, down in the lake, below
'The tiny ripples flame –

'The breeze sings like a summer breeze
'Should sing in summer skies
'And tower-like rocks and tent-like trees
'In mingled glory rise.

10 'But where is he to day, to-day?'
'O question not with me.'
'I will not, Lady, only say
'Where may thy lover be? –

'Is he upon some distant shore
'Or is he on the sea?
'Or the heart thou dost adore
'A faithless heart to thee?'

'The heart I love, whate'er betide
'Is faithful as the grave
20 'And neither foreign lands divide
'Nor yet the rolling wave –'

'Then why should sorrow cloud that brow,
'And tears those eyes bedim?
'Reply this once, is it that thou
'Hast faithless been to him?'

'I gazed upon the cloudless moon
'And loved her all the night
'Till morning came and ardent noon
'Then I forgot her light –

30 'No – not forgot, eternally
'Remains its memory dear;
'But could the day seem dark to me
'Because the night was fair?

'I well may mourn that only one
'Can light my future sky.
'Even though by such a radiant sun
'My moon of life must die' –

Undated

5 *A.G.A. to A.S.*

This summer wind, with thee and me
Roams in the dawn of day;
But thou must be where it shall be,
Ere Evening – far away –

The farewell's echo from thy soul
Should not depart, before
Hills rise and distant rivers roll
Between us evermore –

I know that I have done thee wrong
10   – Have wronged both thee and Heaven –
And I may mourn my lifetime long
Yet may not be forgiven –

Repentant tears will vainly fall
To cancel deeds untrue;
But for no grief can I recall
The dreary word – Adieu –

Yet thou a future peace shalt win
Because thy soul is clear;
And I who had the heart to sin
20   Will find a heart to bear –

Till far beyond earth's frenzied strife,
That makes destruction joy
Thy perished faith shall spring to life
And my remorse shall die

March 2d 1844

6 *A.G.A. to A.S.*

O wander not so far away!
O love, forgive this selfish tear.
It may be sad for thee to stay
But how can I live lonely here

The still May morn is warm and bright
Young flowers look fresh and grass is green
And in the haze of glorious light
Our long low hills are scarcely seen –

The woods – even now their small leaves hide
10 The blackbird and the stockdove well
And high in heaven so blue and wide
A thousand strains of music swell –

He looks on all with eyes that speak
So deep, so drear a woe to me!
There is a faint red on his cheek
Not like the bloom I used to see.

Can Death – yes, Death, he is thine own!
The grave must close those limbs around
And hush, for ever hush the tone
20 I loved above all earthly sound.

Well, pass away with the other flowers
Too dark for them, too dark for thee
Are the hours to come, the joyless hours
That Time is treasuring up for me –

If thou hast sinned in this world of care
'Twas but the dust of thy drear abode –
Thy soul was pure when it entered here
And pure it will go again to God –

May 20th 1838

7 *A.G.A.   To the bluebell —*

Sacred watcher, wave thy bells!
Fair hill flower and woodland child!
Dear to me in deep green dells –
Dearest on the mountains wild –

Bluebell, even as all divine
I have seen my darling shine –
Bluebell, even as wan and frail
I have seen my darling fail –
Thou hast found a voice for me –
10   And soothing words are breathed by thee
–

Thus they murmur, 'Summer's sun
'Warms me till my life is done –
'Would I rather choose to die
'Under winter's ruthless sky?

'Glad I bloom – and calm I fade
'Weeping twilight dews my bed
'Mourner, mourner dry thy tears.
Sorrow comes with lengthened years!'

May 9th 1839 –

8 *Written in Aspin Castle*

How do I love on summer nights
To sit within this Norman door
Whose sombre portal hides the lights
Thickening above me evermore!

How do I love to hear the flow
Of Aspin's water murmuring low
And hours long listen to the breeze
That sighs in Beckden's waving trees

To-night, there is no wind to wake
10   One ripple on the lonely lake.
To-night the clouds subdued and grey
Starlight and moonlight shut away

'Tis calm and still and almost drear
So utter is the solitude;
But still I love to linger here

And form my mood to nature's mood –

There's a wild walk beneath the rocks
Following the bend of Aspin's side
'Tis worn by feet of mountain-flocks
20 That wander down to drink the tide

Never by cliff and gnarled tree
Wound fairy path so sweet to me
Yet of the native shepherds none
In open day and cheerful sun
Will tread its labyrinths alone

Far less, when evening's pensive hour
Hushes the bird and shuts the flower
And gives to Fancy magic power
O'er each familiar tone.

30 For round their hearths they'll tell this tale
And every listener swears it true
How wanders there a phantom pale
With spirit-eyes of dreamy blue –

It always walks with head declined
Its long curls move not in the wind
Its face is fair – divinely fair,
But brooding on that angel brow
Rests such a shade of deep despair
As nought divine could ever know

40 How oft in twilight lingering lone
I've stood to watch that phantom rise
And seen in mist and moonlit stone
Its gleaming hair and solemn eyes

The ancient men in secret say
'Tis the first chief of Aspin grey
That haunts his feudal home

But why – around that alien grave
Three thousand miles beyond the wave –
Where his exiled ashes lie
50 Under the cope of England's sky –
Doth he not rather roam?

I've seen his picture in the hall,
It hangs upon an eastern wall
And often when the sun declines

That picture like an angel shines –

And when the moonbeam chill and blue
Streams the spectral windows through
That picture's like a spectre too –

The hall is full of portraits rare;
60   Beauty and mystery mingle there –
At his right hand an infant fair
Looks from its golden frame.

And just like his its ringlets bright
It(s) large dark eye of shadowy light
Its cheek's pure hue, its forehead white
And like its noble name –

Daughter divine! and could his gaze
Fall coldly on thy peerless face?
And did he never smile to see
70   Himself restored to infancy?

Never part back that golden flow
Of curls – and kiss that pearly brow
And feel no other earthly bliss
Was equal to that parent's kiss?

No – turn towards the western side
There stands Sidonia's deity!
In all her glory, all her pride!
And truly like a god she seems
Some god of wild enthusiast's dreams
80   And this is she for whom he died!
For whom his spirit unforgiven,
Wanders unsheltered shut from heaven
An out cast for eternity –

Those eyes are dust – those lips are clay.
That form is mouldered all away
Nor thought, nor sense, nor pulse, nor breath
The whole devoured and lost in death!

There is no worm however mean,
That living, is not nobler now
90   Than she – Lord Alfred's idol queen
So loved – so worshipped, long ago –

O come away! the Norman door
Is silvered with a sudden shine –
Come leave these dreams o'er things of yore
And turn to Nature's face divine –

O'er wood and wold, o'er flood and fell
O'er flashing lake and gleaming dell
The harvest moon looks down

And when heaven smiles with love and light
100 And earth looks back so dazzling bright
In such a scene, on such a night
Earth's children should not frown –

August 20th 1842
February 6th 1843

9 *Douglases Ride*

Well narrower draw the circle round
And hush that organ's solemn sound,
And quench the lamp and stir the fire
To rouse its flickering radiance higher;
Loop up the window's velvet veil
That we may hear the night-wind wail
For wild those gusts and well their chimes
Blend with a song of troubled times –

SONG
What Rider up Gobelrin's glen
10 Has spurred his straining steed,
And fast and far from living men
Has pressed with maddening speed?

I saw his hoof-prints mark the rock
When swift he left the plain
I heard deep down, the echoing shock
Re echo back again.

From cliff to cliff, through rock and heath
That coal-black courser bounds;
Nor heeds the river pent beneath,
20 Nor marks how fierce it sounds.

With streaming hair and forehead bare
And mantle waving wide
His master rides; the eagles there
Soar up on every side:

The goats fly by with timid cry
Their realm so rashly won:
They pause – he still ascends on high
They gaze, but he is gone.

O gallant horse hold on thy course!
30   The road is tracked behind –
Spur, rider, spur, or vain thy force
Death comes on every wind.

Roared thunder loud from that pitchy cloud?
(Brought) it the torrents flow?
Or woke the breeze in the swaying trees
That frown so dark below?

He breathes at last, when the valley is past;
He rests on the grey rock's brow –
What ails thee steed? At thy master's need,
40   Wilt thou prove faithless now?

No, hardly checked, with ears erect,
The charger champed his rein,
Ere his quivering limbs, all foam-beflecked,
Were off like light again –

Hark through the pass, with threatening crash,
Comes on the increasing roar!
But what shall brave the deep, deep wave?
The deadly path before?

Their feet are dyed in a darker tide
50   Who (dare) those dangers drear –
Their breasts have burst through the battle's worst
And why should they tremble here?

Strong hearts they bear and arms as good
To conquer or to fall
They dash into the boiling flood,
They gain the rock's steep wall –

'Now my bold men this one pass more
'This narrow chasm of stone

'And Douglas – for our sovereign's gore
60 'Shall yield us back his own' –

I hear their ever nearing tread
Sound through the granite glen.
There is a tall pine over-head
Laid by the mountain-men

That dizzy bridge which no horse could track,
Has checked the outlaw's way;
There like a wild beast he turns back
And grimly stands at bay.

Why smiles he so when far below
70 He sees the toiling chase:
The ponderous tree sways heavily
And totters from its place –

They raise their eyes for the sunny skies
Are lost in sudden shade,
But Douglas neither shrinks nor flies –
He need not fly the dead –

July 11th 1838

10 *By R. Gleneden*

From our evening fireside now,
Merry laugh and cheerful tone,
Smiling eye and cloudless brow,
Mirth and music all are flown:

Yet the grass before the door
Grows as green in April rain;
And as blithely as of yore
Larks have poured their day-long strain.

Is it fear, or is it sorrow
10 Checks the stagnant stream of joy?
Do we tremble that tomorrow
May our present peace destroy?

For past misery are we weeping?
What is past can hurt no more;
And the gracious Heavens are keeping
Aid for that which lies before –

One is absent, and for one
Cheerless, chill is our hearthstone –
One is absent, and for him
20   Cheeks are pale and eyes are dim –

Arthur, brother, Gondal's shore
Rested from the battle's roar –
Arthur, brother, we returned
Back to Desmond lost and mourned:

Thou didst purchase by thy fall
Home for us and peace for all;
Yet, how darkly dawned that day –
Dreadful was the price to pay!

Just as once, through sun and mist
30   I have climbed the mountain's breast
Still my gun with certain aim
Brought to earth the fluttering game:

But the very dogs repined,
Though I called with whistle shrill
Listlessly they lagged behind,
Looking backward o'er the hill –

Sorrow was not vocal there;
Mute their pain and my despair
But the joy of life was flown
40   He was gone, and we were lone –

So it is by morn and eve –
So it is in field and hall –
For the absent one we grieve,
One being absent, saddens All –

April 17th 1839 –

11 *Gleneden's Dream*

Tell me, watcher, is it winter?
Say how long my sleep has been?
Have the woods, I left so lovely,
Lost their robes of tender green?

Is the morning slow in coming?
Is the night time loath to go?

Tell me, are the dreary mountains
Drearier still with drifted snow?

'Captive, since thou sawest the forest
10 'All its leaves have died away
'And another March has woven
'Garlands for another May –

'Ice has barred the Artic water,
'Soft south winds have set it free
'And once more to deep green valley
'Golden flowers might welcome thee' –

Watcher, in this lonely prison,
Shut from joy and kindly air
Heaven, descending in a vision
20 Taught my soul to do and bear –

It was night, a night of winter;
I lay on the dungeon floor,
And all other sounds were silent –
All, except the river's roar –

Over Death, and Desolation,
Fireless hearths, and lifeless homes
Over orphans' heart-sick sorrows,
Patriot fathers' bloody tombs;

Over friends that my arms never
30 Might embrace, in love, again –
Memory pondered until madness
Struck its poignard in my brain –

Deepest slumber followed raving,
Yet. methought, I brooded still –
Still I saw my country bleeding,
Dying for a Tyrant's will –

Not because my bliss was blasted
Burned within, the avenging flame –
Not because my scattered kindred
40 Died in woe, or lived in shame.

God doth know, I would have given
Every bosom dear to me
Could that sacrifice have purchased
Tortured Gondal's liberty!

But, that at Ambition's bidding
All her cherished hopes should wane;
That her noblest sons should muster,
Strive, and fight and fall in vain –

Hut and castle, hall and cottage,
500 Roofless, crumbling to the ground –
Mighty Heaven, a glad Avenger
Thy eternal justice found!

Yes, the arm that once would shudder
Even to pierce a wounded deer,
I beheld it, unrelenting,
Choke in blood its sovereign's prayer –

Glorious dream! I saw the city
Blazing in imperial shine;
And, among adoring thousands
60 Stood a man of form divine –

None need point the princely victim
Now he smiles with royal pride!
Now his glance is bright as lightening:
Now – the knife is in his side!

Ha, I saw how Death could darken –
Darken that triumphant eye!
His red heart's blood drenched my dagger;
My ear drank his dying sigh!

Shadows come! What means this midnight?
70 O my God, I know it all!
Know the fever–dream is over,
Unavenged, the Avengers fall!

May 21st 1838

12 *Rosina 2'*

Weeks of wild delirium past –
Weeks of fevered pain,
Rest from suffering comes at last –
Reason dawns again –

It was a pleasant April day
Declining to the afternoon –

Sunshine upon her pillow lay
As warm as middle June.

It told her how unconciously
10   Early spring had hurried by
'Ah Time has not delayed for me!'
She murmured with a sigh.

'Angora's hills have heard their tread
'The crimson flag is planted there –
'Elderno's waves are rolling red,
'While <u>I</u> lie fettered here!

'Nay, rather, Gondal's shaken throne
'Is now secure and free;
'And my King Julius reigns alone,
20   'Debtless, alas to me!'

Loud was the sudden gush of woe
From those who watched around;
Rosina turned and sought to know
Why burst that boding sound.

'What then, my dreams are false,' she said
'Come maidens, answer me –
'Has Almedore in battle fled?
'Have slaves subdued the free?

'I know it all, he could not bear
30   'To leave me dying far away –
'He fondly, madly lingered here
'And we have lost the day!

'But check those coward sobs, and bring
'My robes and smoothe my tangled hair:
'A noble victory you shall sing
'For every hour's despair!

'When will he come? 'Twill soon be night –
'He'll come when evening falls –
'Oh I shall weary for the light
40   'To leave my lonely halls!'

She turned her pallid face aside
As she would seek repose;
But dark Ambition's thwarted pride
Forbade her lids to close –

And still on all who waited by
Oppressive mystery hung,
And swollen with grief, was every eye
And chained was every tongue.

They whispered nought, but, 'Lady, sleep,
50   'Dear Lady, slumber now!
'Had we not bitter cause to weep
'While you were laid so low?

'And Hope can hardly deck the cheek
'With sudden sight of cheer
'When it has worn through many a week
'The stamp of anguish drear.'

Fierce grew Rosina's gloomy gaze
She cried, 'Dissemblers, own
'Exina's arms in victory blaze
60   'Brenzaida's crest is down'

'Well, since it must be told, Lady,
'Brenzaida's crest is down
'Brenzaida's sun is set, Lady,
'His empire over thrown!

'He died beneath this palace dome –
'True hearts on every side –
'Among his guards, within his home
'Our glorious monarch died

'I saw him fall. I saw the gore
70   'From his heart's fountain swell
And, mingling on the marble floor
His murderer's life-blood fell –

'And now, mid northern mountains lone
'His desert grave is made;
'And, Lady, of your love, alone
'Remains a mortal shade!"

September 1st 1841.

13 *Song by Julius Brenzaida to G.S.*

Geraldine, the moon is shining
With so soft, so bright a ray,
Seems it not that eve, declining
Ushered in a fairer day?

While the wind is whispering only,
Far – across the water borne
Let us, in this silence lonely
Sit beneath the ancient thorn –

Wild the road, and rough and dreary;
10   Barren all the moorland round;
Rude the couch that rests us weary;
Mossy stone and heathy ground –

But when winter storms were meeting
In the moonless midnight dome
Did we heed the tempest's beating
Howling round our spirits' home?

No, that thee, with branches riven
Whitening in the whirl of snow,
As it tossed against the heaven,
20   Sheltered happy hearts below –

And at Autumn's mild returning
Shall our feet forget the way?
And in Cynthia's silver morning,
Geraldine, wilt thou delay?

October 17th 1838

14 *Song by J. Brenzaida to G.S.*

I knew not 'twas so dire a crime
To say the word, Adieu:
But, this shall be the only time
My slighted heart shall sue.

The wild moorside, the winter morn,
The gnarled and ancient tree –
If in your breast they waken scorn
Shall wake the same in me.

I can forget black eyes and brows
10   And lips of rosy charm
If you forget the sacred vows
Those faithless lips could form –

If hard commands can tame your love,
Or prison walls can hold
I would not wish to grieve above
A thing so false and cold –

And there are bosoms bound to mine
With links both tried and strong,
And there are eyes, whose lightening shine
20   Has warmed and blessed me long:

Those eyes shall make my only day,
Shall set my spirit free
And chase the foolish thoughts away
That mourn your memory!

October 17 1838.

15 *Geraldine*

'Twas night, her comrades gathered all
Within their city's rocky wall,
When flowers were closed and day was o'er
Their joyous hearts awoke the more

But lonely, in her distant cave
She heard the river's restless wave
Chafing its banks with dreamy flow,
Music for mirth, and wail for woe –

Palmtrees and cedars towering high
10   Deepened the gloom of evening's sky
And thick did raven ringlets veil
Her forehead, drooped like lily pale

Yet I could hear my lady sing;
I knew she did not mourn,
For never yet from sorrow's spring
Such witching notes were born

Thus poured she in that cavern wild
The voice of feelings warm

As, bending o'er her beauteous child
20 She clasped its sleeping form –

'Why sank so soon the summer sun
'From our Zedora's skies?
'I was not tired, my darling one,
'Of gazing in thine eyes –

'Methought the heaven whence thou hast come
'Was lingering there awhile
'And Earth seemed such an alien home
'They did not dare to smile.

'Methought each moment, something strange
30 'Within their circles shone
'And yet, through every magic change
'They were Brenzaida's own.

'Methought – What thought I not, sweet love?
'My whole heart centered there;
'I breathed not but to send above
'One gush of ardent prayer.

'Bless it, my gracious God,' I cried,
'Preserve thy mortal shrine
'For thine own sake, be thou its guide
40 'And keep it still divine!

'Say, sin shall never blanche that cheek
'Nor suffering change that brow
'Speak, in thy mercy maker, speak,
'And seal it safe from woe!'

'Why did I doubt? In God's control
'Our mutual fates remain
'And pure as now, my angel's soul
'<u>Must</u> go to heaven again.'

The revellers in the city slept,
50 My lady, in her woodland bed;
<u>I</u>, watching o'er her slumber wept
As one who mourns the dead!

August 17th 1841

16 *A.G.A.*

For him who struck thy foreign string
I ween this heart hast ceased to care
Then why dost thou such feelings bring
To my sad spirit, old guitar?

It is as if the warm sunlight
In some deep glen should lingering stay
When clouds of tempest and of night
Had wrapt the parent orb away –

It is as if the glassy brook
10   Should image still its willows fair
Though years ago, the woodman's stroke
Laid low in dust their gleaming hair:

Even so, guitar, thy magic tone
Hast moved the tear and waked the sigh
Hast bid the ancient torrent flow
Although its very source is dry!

August 30th 1838

17 *F. De Samara Written in the Gaaldine prison caves To A.G.A.*

Thy sun is near meridian height
And my sun sinks in endless night;
But if that night bring only sleep
Then I shall rest, while thou wilt weep.

And say not, that my early tomb
Will give me to a darker doom.
Shall these long agonising years
Be punished by eternal tears?

No, that I feel can never be;
10   A God of hate could hardly bear
To watch, through all eternity,
His own creations' dread despair!

The pangs that wring my mortal breast
Must claim from Justice, lasting rest:
Enough, that this departing breath
Will pass in anguish worse than death.

If I have sinned, long, long ago
That sin was purified by woe –
I've suffered on through night and day;
20   I've trod a dark and frightful way:

Earth's wilderness was round me spread
Heaven's tempests beat my naked head –
I did not kneel – in vain would prayer
Have sought one gleam of mercy there!

How could I ask for pitying love
When that grim concave frowned above
Hoarding its lightenings to destroy
My only and my priceless joy?

They struck – and long may Eden shine
30   Ere I would call its glories mine
All Heaven's undreamt felicity
Could never blot the past from me –

No, years may cloud and death may sever
But what is done, is done for ever –
And thou false friend, and treacherous guide,
Go sate thy cruel heart with pride –

Go, load my memory with shame;
Speak but to curse my hated name:
My tortured limbs in dungeons bind
40   And spare my life to kill my mind –

Leave me in chains and darkness now
And when my very soul is worn,
When reason's light has left my brow
And madness cannot feel thy scorn,

Then come again – thou wilt not shrink;
I know thy soul is free from fear
The last full cup of triumph drink,
Before the blank of death be there –

Thy raving, dying victim see;
50   Lost, cursed, degraded all for thee!
Gaze on the wretch – recall to mind
His golden days left long behind –

Does memory sleep in Lethian rest?
Or wakes its whisper in thy breast?

O memory, wake! let scenes return
That even her haughty heart must mourn!

Reveal, where o'er a lone green wood
The moon of summer pours
Far down from heaven, its silver flood
60 On deep Elderno's shores –

There, lingering in the wild embrace
Youth's warm affections gave
She sits, and fondly seems to trace
His features in the wave –

And while, on that reflected face
Her eyes intently dwell:
'Fernando, sing to-night', she says,
'The lays I love so well.'

He smiles and sings though every air
70 Betrays the faith of yesterday:
His soul is glad to cast for her
Virtue and Faith and Heaven away –

Well, thou hast paid me back my love!
But, if there be a God above
Whose arm is strong, whose word is true
This hell shall wring thy spirit too!

January 6th 1840.

18 *F. De Samara to A.G.A.*

Light up thy halls! 'Tis closing day;
I'm drear and lone and far away –
Cold blows on my breast, the northwind's bitter sigh
And oh, my couch is bleak beneath the rainy sky!

Light up thy halls – and think not of me;
That face is absent now, thou has hated so to see –
Bright be thine eyes, undimmed their dazzling shine,
For never, never more shall they encounter mine!

The desert moor is dark; there is tempest in the air:
10 I have breathed my only wish in one last, one burning prayer –
A prayer that would come forth, although it lingered long:
That set on fire my heart, but froze upon my tongue –

And now, it shall be done before the morning rise:
I will not watch the sun ascend in yonder skies,
One task alone remains – thy pictured face to view
And then I go to prove if God, at least, be true!

Do I not see thee now? Thy black resplendent hair;
Thy glory-beaming brow, and smile how heavenly fair!
Thine eyes are turned away – those eyes I would not see:
20 Their dark, their deadly ray would more than madden me

There, go, Deceiver, go! my hand is streaming wet;
My heart's blood flows to buy the blessing – To forget!
Oh could that lost heart give back, back again to thine
One tenth part of the pain that clouds my dark decline!

Oh could I see thy lids weighed down in cheerless woe;
Too full to hide their tears, too stern to overflow;
Oh could I know thy soul with equal grief was torn –
This fate might be endured – this anguish might be borne!

How gloomy grows the Night! 'Tis Gondal's wind that blows
30 I shall not tread again the deep glens where it rose –
I feel it on my face – where, wild blast, dost thou roam?
What do we, wanderer, here? So far away from home?

I do not need thy breath to cool my death-cold brow
But go to that far land where She is shining now;
Tell Her my latest wish, tell Her my dreary doom;
Say, that my pangs are past, but Hers are yet to come –

Vain words – vain, frenzied thoughts! No ear can hear me call –
Lost in the vacant air my frantic curses fall –
And could she see me now, perchance her lip would smile
40 Would smile in careless pride and utter scorn the while!

And yet, for all Her hate, each parting glance would tell
A stronger passion breathed, burned in this last farewell –
Unconquered in my soul the Tyrant rules me still –
Life bows to my control, but, Love I cannot kill!

November 1st 1838

19 *Written on returning to the P. of I.*
on the 10th of January 1827

The busy day has hurried by
And hearts greet kindred hearts once more
And swift the evening hours should fly
But – what turns every gleaming eye
So often to the door?

And then so quick away – and why
Does sudden silence chill the room?
And laughter sinks into a sigh –
And merry words to whispers die –
10   And gladness change to gloom?

O we are listening for a sound
We know, shall ne'er be heard again
Sweet voices in the halls resound;
Fair forms, fond faces gather round,
But all in vain – in vain!

Their feet shall never waken more
The echoes in these galleries wide,
Nor dare the snow on the mountain's brow,
Nor skim the river's frozen flow,
20   Nor wander down its side –

They who have been our Life – our soul –
Through summer-youth, from childhood's spring –
Who bound us in one vigorous whole
To stand 'gainst Tyranny's control
For ever triumphing –

Who bore the brunt of battle's fray
The first to fight, the last to fall
Whose mighty minds – with kindred ray
Still led the van in Glory's way –
30   The idol chiefs of all –

They, they are gone! not for a while
As golden suns at night decline
And even in death our grief beguile
Foretelling, with a rose-red smile,
How bright the morn will shine –

No these dark towers are lone and lorn;
This very crowd is vacancy:
And we must watch and wait and mourn

And half look out for their return;
40   And think their forms we see –

And fancy music in our ear
Such as their lips could only pour
And think we feel their presence near
And start to find they are not here
And never shall be more!

June 14th 1839

20 *On the fall of Zalona*

All blue and bright, in glorious light
The morn comes marching on.
And now Zalona's steeples white
Glow golden in the sun –

This day might be a festal day;
The streets are crowded all,
And emerald flags stream broad and gay
From turret, tower and wall;

And hark! how music, evermore
10   Is sounding in the sky:
The deep bells boom – the cannon roar,
The trumpets sound on high –

The deep bells boom, the deep bells clash
Upon the reeling air:
The cannon, with unceasing crash
Make answer far and near –

What do those brazen tongues proclaim?
What joyous fête begun –
What offering to our country's fame –
20   What noble victory won?

Go ask that solitary Sire
Laid in his house alone;
His silent hearth without a fire –
His sons and daughters gone –

Go, ask those children, in the street
Beside their mother's door;
Waiting to hear the lingering feet
That they shall hear no more –

Ask those pale soldiers round the gates
30   With famine-kindled eye –
They'll say, 'Zalona celebrates
The day that she must die!

The charger, by his manger tied
Has rested many a day;
Yet ere the spur have touched his side,
Behold, he sinks away!

And hungry dogs, with wolf-like cry
Unburied corpses tear;
While their gaunt masters gaze and sigh
40   And scarce the feast forbear –

Now, look down from Zalona's wall –
There, war the unwearied foe:
If ranks before our cannon fall,
New ranks, forever, grow –

And many a week, unbroken thus,
Their troops, our ramparts hem;
And for each man that fights for us
And hundred fight for them!

Courage and Right and Spotless Truth
50   Were pitched 'gainst traitorous crime
We offered all – our age, our youth –
Our brave men in their prime –

And all have failed! the fervent prayers,
The trust in heavenly aid,
Valour and Faith and sealed tears
That would not mourn the dead –

Lips, that did breathe no murmuring word;
Hearts, that did ne'er complain
Though vengeance held a sheathed sword
60   And martyrs bled in vain –

Alas, alas, the Myrtle bowers
By blighting blasts destroyed!
Alas, the Lily's withered flowers
That leave the garden void!

Unfolds o'er tower, and waves o'er height
A sheet of crimson sheen –

Is it the setting sun's red light
That stains our standard green?

Heaven help us in this awful hour!
70   For now might Faith decay –
Now might we doubt God's guardian power
And curse, instead of pray –

He will not even let us die –
Not let us die at home;
The foe must see our soldiers fly
As they had feared the tomb:

Because, we <u>dare</u> not stay to gain
Those longed for, glorious graves –
We dare not shrink from slavery's chain
80   To leave our children slaves!

But when this scene of awful woe
Has neared its final close
As God forsook our armies, so
May He forsake our foes!

February 24th 1843.

21 *A.G.A. The Death of*

Were they shepherds, who sat all day
On that brown mountain-side?
But neither staff nor dog had they:
Nor woolly flock to guide –

They were clothed in savage attire:
Their locks were dark and long:
And at each belt a weapon dire,
Like bandit-knife was hung –

One was a woman tall and fair;
10   A princess she might be
From her stately form and her features rare
And her look of majesty.

But oh, she had a sullen frown –
A lip of cruel scorn –
As sweet tears never melted down
Her cheeks since she was born!

'Twas well she had no sceptre to wield,
No subject land to sway;
Fear might have made her vassals yield,
20   But Love had been far away –

Yet, Love was even at her feet
In his most burning mood –
That Love, which will the Wicked greet
As kindly as the Good –

And he was noble too, who bowed
So humbly by her side –
Entreating, till his eyes o'erflowed,
Her spirit's icy pride –

'Angelica, from my very birth
30   'I have been nursed in strife,
'And lived upon this weary Earth
'A wanderer, all my life:

'The baited tiger could not be
'So much athirst for gore,
'For men and Laws have tortured me
'Till I can bear no more –

'The guiltless blood upon my hands
'Will shut me out from heaven
'And here, and even in foreign lands,
40   'I cannot find a haven –

'And in all space, and in all time,
'And through Eternity,
'To aid a spirit lost in crime,
'I have no hope but thee –

'Yet will I swear, No saint on high
'A truer faith could prove –
'No angel, from that holy sky,
'Could give thee purer love!

'For thee, through never-ending years
50   'I'd suffer endless pain;
'But – only give me back my tears
'Return my love again!'

Many a time, unheeded, thus
The reckless man would pray;
But something woke an answering flush

On his lady's brow to-day,
And her eye flashed flame, as she turned to speak,
In concord with her reddening cheek –

'I've known a hundred kinds of Love –
60   'All, made the loved one rue;
'And what is thine that it should prove,
'Than other love, more true?

'Listen, I've known a burning heart
'To which my own was given
'Nay, not in passion, do not start –
'Our love was love from heaven:
'At least if heavenly love be born
'In the pure light of childhood's morn
'Long ere the poison-tainted air
70   'From this world's plague-fen rises there:

'That heart was like a tropic sun
'That kindles all it shines upon;
'And never Magian devotee
'Gave worship half so warm as (I);
'And never glittering bow could be
'So welcome in a stormy sky
'My soul dwelt with her day and night
'She was my all sufficing light –
'My childhood's mate, my girlhood's guide,
80   'My only blessing, only pride.

'But cursed be the very earth
'That gave that fiend her fatal birth!
'With her own hand she bent the bow
'That laid my best affections low.
'Then mocked my grief and scorned my prayers
'And drowned my bloom of youth in tears –
'Warnings, reproaches, both were vain;
'What recked she of another's pain?
'My dearer self she would not spare –
90   'From Honour's voice, she turned his ear;
'First made her love his only stay;
'Then snatched the treacherous prop away!
'Douglas, he pleaded bitterly –
'He pleaded, as you plead to me,
'For life-long chains or timeless tomb
'Or any, but an Exile's doom:
'We both were scorned – both sternly driven
'To shelter 'neath a foreign heaven;
'And darkens o'er that dreary time

100   'A wildering dream of frenzied crime.
'I would not now those days recall;
'The oath within the caverned hall
'And its fulfilment, those you know:
'We both together struck the blow:
'But – you can never know the pain
'That my lost heart did‘then sustain
'When, severed wide by guiltless gore,
'I felt that <u>one</u> could love no more!
'Back maddening thought! – The grave is deep
110   'Where my Amedeus lies asleep,
'And I have long forgot to weep –

'Now hear me, in these regions wild
'I saw to-day my enemy
'Unarmed, as helpless as a child
'She slumbered on a sunny lea;
'Two Friends, no other guard had she;
'And they were wandering on the braes;
'And chasing, in regardless glee,
'The wild goat o'er his dangerous ways –

120   'My hand was raised – my knife was bare:
'With stealthy tread I stole along
'But a wild bird sprang from his hidden lair
'And woke her with a sudden song:
'Yet moved she not; she only raised
'Her lids and on the bright sun gazed
'And uttered such a dreary sigh
'I thought, just then she should not die
'Since living was such misery –

'Now Douglas, for our hunted band –
130   'For future joy and former woe,
'Assist me, with thy heart and hand
'To send to hell my mortal foe –
'Her friends fell first, that she may drain
'A deeper cup of bitterer pain;
'Yonder they stand and watch the waves
'Dash in among the echoing caves –
'Their farewell sight of earth and sea:
'Come, Douglas, rise and go with me –'

                    *   *   *

The lark sang clearly overhead
140   And sweetly hummed the bee

And softly, round their dying bed,
The wind blew from the sea –

Fair Surry would have raised her eyes
To see that water shine:
To see once more, in mountain skies
The summer sun decline:

But ever, on her fading cheek,
The languid lid would close
As weary that such light should break
150 Its much-desired repose.

And she was waning fast away –
Even Memory's voice grew dim;
Her former life's eventful day
Had dwindled to a dream;

And hardly could her mind recall
One thought of joy or pain;
That cloud was gathering over all
Which never clears again:

In vain – in vain, you need not gaze
160 Upon those features now!
That sinking head you need not raise,
Nor kiss that pulseless brow –

Let out the grief that chokes your breath;
Lord Lesley, set it free:
The sternest eye, for such a death
Might fill with sympathy.

The tresses o'er her bosom spread
Were by a faint breeze blown;
'Her heart is beating,' Lesley said,
170 'She is not really gone!'

And still that form he fondly pressed,
And still of hope he dreamed
Nor marked, how from his own young breast
Life's crimson current streamed –

At last, the sunshine left the ground,
The laden bee flew home,
The deepdown sea, with sadder sound
Impelled its waves to foam;

And the corpse grew heavy on his arm,
180   The starry heaven grew dim;
The summer night so mild and warm,
Felt wintry chill to him.

A troubled shadow, o'er his eye
Came down, and rested there;
The moors and sky went swimming by
Confused and strange and drear

He faintly prayed, 'Oh, Death, delay
'Thy last fell dart to throw
'Till I can hear my sovereign say,
190   'The traitors' heads are low!

'God, guard her life, since not to me
'That dearest boon was given:
'God, bless her arm with victory
'Or bless not me with heaven!'

Then came the cry of agony;
The pang of parting pain;
And he had overpassed the sea
That none can pass again –

*   *   *

Douglas leaned above the well;
200   Heather banks around him rose;
Bright and warm the sunshine fell
On that spot of sweet repose –

With the blue heaven bending o'er,
And the soft wind singing by
And the clear stream, evermore
Mingling harmony –

On the shady side reclined,
He watched its waters play
And sound and sight had well combined
210   To banish gloom away –

A voice spoke near – 'She'll come', it said,
'And, Douglas, thou shalt be
'My love, although the very dead
'Should rise to rival thee!

'Now only let thine arm be true
'And nerved, like mine, to kill;
'And Gondal's royal race shall rue
'This day on Elmor Hill!' –

They wait not long, the rustling heath
220   Betrays their royal foe;
With hurried step and panting breath
And cheek almost as white as death,
Augusta sprang below –

Yet marked she not where Douglas lay
She only saw the well;
The tiny fountain, churning spray
Within its mossy cell –

'Oh, I have wrongs to pay', she cried,
'Give life, give vigour now!'
230   And, stooping by the water's side,
She drank its crystal flow.

And brightly, with that draught, came back
The glory of her matchless eye
As, glancing o'er the moorland track,
She shook her head impatiently –

Nor shape, nor shade – the mountain flocks
Quietly feed in grassy dells;
Nor sound, except the distant rocks
Echoing to their bells –

240   She turns – she meets the murderer's gaze:
Her own is scorched with a sudden blaze –
The blood streams down her brow;

The blood streams through her coal-black hair –
She strikes it off with little care;
She scarcely feels it flow,

For she has marked and known him too
And his own heart's ensanguined dew
Must slake her vengeance now!

False Friend! no tongue save thine can tell
250   The mortal strife that then befell:

But, ere night darkened down
The stream in silence sang once more
And, on its green bank, bathed in gore
Augusta lay alone!

False Love! no earthly eye did see,
Yet Heaven's pure eye regarded thee
Where thy own Douglas bled –
How thou didst turn in mockery
From his last hopeless agony
260   And leave the hungry hawk to be
Sole watcher of the dead!

*   *   *

Was it a deadly swoon?
Or was her spirit really gone;
And the cold corpse, beneath the moon
Laid like another mass of dust and stone?

The moon was full that night.
The sky was almost light like day:
You might have seen the pulse's play
Upon her forehead white;

270   You might have seen the dear, dear sign of life
In her uncovered eye
And her cheek changing in the mortal strife
Betwixt the pain to live and agony to die –

But nothing mutable was there!
The face, all deadly fair,
Showed a fixed impress of keen suffering past,
And the raised lid did show
No wandering gleam below
But a stark anguish, self-destroyed at last –

280   Long he gazed and held his breath,
Kneeling on the blood-stained heath:
Long he gazed those lids beneath
Looking into death!

Not a word from his followers fell,
They stood by mute and pale;
That black treason uttered well
Its own heart-harrowing tale –

But earth was bathed in other gore;
There were crimson drops across the moor
290 And Lord Eldred, glancing round
Saw those tokens on the ground:

'Bring him back!' he hoarsly said,
'Wounded is the traitor fled,
'Vengeance may hold but minutes brief
'And you have all your lives for grief.'

He is left alone – he sees the stars
Their quiet ourse continuing
And, far away, down Elmor scars
He hears the stream its waters fling:

300 That lulling monotone did sing
Of broken rock and shaggy glen.
Of welcome for the moorcock's wing,
But, not of wail for men!

Nothing in heaven or earth to show
One sign of sympathising woe –
And nothing but that agony
In her now unconcious eye
To weigh upon the labouring breast
And prove she did not pass at rest –

310 But he who watched, in thought had gone
Retracing back her lifetime flown;
Like sudden ghosts, to memory came
Full many a face, and many a name,
Full many a heart, that in the tomb,
He almost deemed, might have throbbed again
Had they but known her dreary doom,
Had they but seen their idol there,
A wreck of desolate despair,
Left to the wild birds of the air
320 And mountain winds and rain!
For him – no tear his stern eye shed
As he looked down upon the dead –

'Wild morn, he thought, – and doubtful noon;
'But, yet it was a glorious sun
'Though comet-like its course was run:
'That sun should never have been given

'To burn and dazzle in the heaven
'Or, night has quenched it far too soon!
'And thou art gone – with all thy pride,
330   'Thou, so adored, so deified!
'Cold as the earth, unweeting now
'Of love, or joy, or mortal woe –

'For what thou wert, I would not grieve,
'But much for what thou wert to be –
That life, so stormy and so brief,
'That death, has wronged us more than thee!
'Thy passionate youth was nearly past
'The opening sea seemed smooth at last
'Yet vainly flowed the calmer wave
340   'Since fate had not decreed to save –
'And vain too must the sorrow be
'Of those who live to mourn for thee:
'But Gondal's foes shall not complain
'That thy dear blood was poured in vain!'

January, 1841 –
May, 1844 –

22 *A Farewell to Alexandria*

I've seen this dell in July's shine
As lovely as an angel's dream;
Above, heaven's depth of blue divine:
Around, the evening's golden beam –

I've seen the purple heather-bell
Look out by many a storm-worn stone
And oh, I've known such music swell,
Such wild notes wake these passes lone –

So soft, yet so intensely felt –
So low, yet so distinctly heard
My breath would pause, my eyes would melt
And my tears dew the green heath-sward –

I'd linger here a summer day
Nor care how fast the hours flew by
Nor mark the sun's departing ray
Smile sadly glorious from the sky

Then, then I might have laid thee down
And deemed thy sleep would gentle be
I might have left thee, darling one
And thought thy God was guarding thee!

But now, there is no wandering glow
No gleam to say that God is nigh:
And coldly spreads thy couch of snow
And harshly sounds thy lullaby.

Forests of heather dark and long
Wave their brown branching arms above
And they must soothe thee with their song
And they must shield my child of love!

Alas the flakes are heavily falling
They cover fast each guardian crest:
And chilly white their shroud is palling
Thy frozen limbs and freezing breast –

Wakes up the storm more madly wild
The mountain drifts are tossed on high –
Farewell unblessed, unfriended child,
I cannot bear to watch thee die!

July 12th 1839

23 *E.W. to A.G.A.*

How few, of all the hearts that loved,
Are grieving for thee now!
And why should mine, to-night, be moved
With such a sense of woe?

Too often, thus, when left alone
Where none my thoughts can see,
Comes back a word, a passing tone
From thy strange history.

Sometimes I seem to see thee rise
A glorious child again –
All virtues beaming from thine eyes
That ever honoured men –

Courage and Truth, a generous breast
Where Love and Gladness lay;
A being whose very Memory blest
And made the mourner gay –

O, fairly spread thy early sail
And fresh and pure and free
Was the first impulse of the gale
That urged life's wave for thee!

Why did the pilot, too confiding
Dream o'er that Ocean's foam,
And trust in Pleasure's careless guiding
To bring his vessel home?

For, well, he knew what dangers frowned,
What mists would gather dim,
What rocks and shelves and sands lay round
Between his port and him –

The very brightness of the sun,
The splendour of the main,
The wind that bore him wildly on
Should not have warned in vain

An anxious gazer from the shore,
I marked the whitening wave
And wept above thy fate the more
Because I could not save –

It recks not now, when all is over,
But, yet my heart will be
A mourner still, though friend and lover
40 Have both forgotten thee!

March 11th. 1844.

24

Come, walk with me,
There's only thee
To bless my spirit now –
We used to love on winter nights
To wander through the snow;
Can we not woo back old delights?
The clouds rush dark and wild
They fleck with shade our mountain height,
The same as long ago
10 And on the horizon rest at last
In looming masses piled;
While moonbeams flash and fly so fast
We scarce can say they smiled.

Come walk with me, come walk with me:
We were not once so few
But Death has stolen our company
As sunshine steals the dew –
He took them one by one and we
Are left the only two;
20 So closer would my feelings twine
Because they have no stay but thine –

'Nay call me not it may not be
'Is human love so true?
'Can Friendship's flower droop on for years
'And then revive anew?
'No, though the soil be wet with tears
'How fair so e'er it grew
'The vital sap once perished
'Will never flow again
30 'And surer than that dwelling dread,
'The narrow dungeon of the Dead,
'Time parts the hearts of men –'

Undated

25 *Date 18– E.G. to M.R.*

Thy Guardians are asleep
So I've come to bid thee rise,
Thou hast a holy vow to keep
Ere yon crescent quit the skies:

Though clouds careering wide
Will hardly let her gleam
She's bright enough to be our guide
Across the mountain stream.

O waken, Dearest, wake!
What means this long delay?
Say, wilt thou not for honour's sake
Chase idle fears away?

Think not of future grief
Entailed on present joy:
An age of woe were only brief
Its memory to destroy –

And neither Hell nor Heaven
Though both conspire at last
Can take the bliss that has been given –
Can rob us of the past –

Then waken, Mary, wake
How canst thou linger now?
For true love's and Gleneden's sake,
Arise and keep thy vow!

May 4th 1843

26 *To A.S. 1830*

Where beams the sun the brightest
In the hours of sweet July?
Where falls the snow the lightest
From bleak December's sky?

Where can the weary lay his head
And lay it safe the while
In a grave that never shuts its dead
From heaven's benignant smile?

Upon the earth in sunlight
10   Spring grass grows green and fair
But beneath the earth is midnight –
Eternal midnight there!

Then why lament that those we love
Escape Earth's dungeon tomb?
As if the flowers that blow above
Could charm its undergloom –

From morning's faintest dawning
Till Evening's deepest shade
Thou wilt not cease thy mourning
20   To know where she is laid;

But if to weep above her grave
Be such a priceless boon
Go, shed thy tears in ocean's wave
And they will reach it soon.

Yet midst thy wild repining
Mad though that anguish be
Think heaven on her is shining
Even as it shines on thee –

With thy mind's vision pierce the Deep
30   Look how she rests below
And tell me, why such blessed sleep
Should cause such bitter woe?

May 1st 1843

27

In the earth, the earth thou shalt be laid
A grey stone standing over thee;
Black mould beneath thee spread
And black mould to cover thee.

'Well, there is rest there,
'So fast come thy prophecy –
'The time when my sunny hair
'Shall with grass roots twined be'

But cold, cold is that resting place
10   Shut out from Joy and Liberty
And (all) who loved thy living face
Will shrink from its gloom and thee

'Not so, <u>here</u> the world is chill
'And sworn Friends fall from me
'But <u>there</u>, they'll own me still
'And prize my memory'

Farewell then, all that love,
All that deep sympathy:
Sleep on, heavens laugh above
20   Earth never misses thee –

Turf-sod and tombstone drear
Part human company.
One heart broke, only, there –
<u>That</u> heart was worthy thee! –

September 6th 1843

28 *A.S. to G.S. . . .*

I do not weep, I would not weep;
Our Mother needs no tears:
Dry thine eyes too, 'tis vain to keep
This causeless grief for years

What though her brow be changed and cold.
Her sweet eyes closed for ever?
What though the stone – the darksome mould
Our mortal bodies sever?

What though her hand smoothe ne'er again
10   Those silken locks of thine –
Nor through long hours of future pain
Her kind face o'er thee shine?

Remember still she is not dead
She sees us, Gerald, now,
Laid where her angel spirit fled
'Mid heath and frozen snow

And from that world of heavenly light
Will she not always bend,
To guide us in our lifetime's night
20   And guard us to the end?

Thou knowst she will and well mayst mourn
That we are left below
But not that she can ne'er return
To share our earthly woe –

December 19th 1841.

29 *M.G. for the U.S.*

'Twas yesterday at early dawn
I watched the falling snow:
A drearier scene on winter morn
Was never stretched below –

I could not see the mountains round
But I knew by the wind's wild roar
How every drift in their glens profound
Was deepening ever more –

And then I thought of Ula's bowers
10   Beyond the Southern Sea
Her tropic prairies bright with flowers
And rivers wandering free –

I thought of many a happy day
Spent in her Eden isle
With my dear comrades young and gay
All scattered now so far away
But not forgot the while!

Who that has breathed that heavenly air
To northern climes would come
20   To Gondal's mists and moorlands drear
And sleet and frozen gloom?

Spring brings the swallow and the lark
But what will winter bring?
Its twilight hours and evenings dark
To match the gifts of Spring?

No, look with me o'er that sullen main
If thy spirit's eye can see
There are brave ships floating back again
That no calm southern port could chain
30   From Gondal's stormy sea

O how the hearts of the voyagers beat
To feel the frost-wind blow!
What flower in Ula's gardens sweet
Is worth one flake of snow?

The blast which almost rends their sail
Is welcome as a friend;
It brings them home, that thundering gale
Home to their journey's end:

Home to our souls whose wearying sighs
40   Lament their absence drear
And feel how bright even winter skies
Would shine if they were here!

December 19th 1843

30

The linnet in the rocky dells,
The moorlark in the air,
The bee among the heather bells
That hide my lady fair –

The wild deer browse above her breast:
The wild birds raise their brood.
And they, her smiles of love caressed,
Have left her solitude!

I ween, that when the grave's dark wall
10   Did first her form retain
They thought their hearts could ne'er recall
The light of joy again –

They thought the tide of grief would flow
Unchecked through future years
But where is all their anguish now,
And where are all their tears?

Well, let them fight for Honour's breath
Or Pleasure's shade pursue –
The Dweller in the land of Death
20   Is changed and careless too –

And if their eyes should watch and weep
Till sorrows' source were dry
She would not, in her tranquil sleep,
Return a single sigh –

Blow, west wind, by the lonely mound
And murmur, summer streams,
There is no need of other sound
To soothe my Lady's dreams –

EW   May 1st 1844

31 *JB. Sept. 1825 –*
From a Dungeon Wall in the Southern College –

'Listen! when your hair like mine
'Takes a tint of silver grey,
'When your eyes, with dimmer shine,
'Watch life's bubbles float away,

'When you, young man, have borne like me
'The weary weight of sixty three
'Then shall penance sore be paid
'For these hours so wildly squandered
'And the words that now fall dead
10   'On your ears be deeply pondered
'Pondered and approved at last
'But their virtue will be past!

'Glorious is the prize of Duty
'Though she be a serious power
'Treacherous all the lures of Beauty
'Thorny bud and poisonous flower!

'Mirth is but a mad beguiling
'Of the golden gifted Time –
'Love – a demon meteor wiling
20   'Heedless feet to gulfs of crime.

'Those who follow earthly pleasure,
'Heavenly knowledge will not lead
'Wisdom hides from them her treasure,
'Virtue bids them evil speed!

'Vainly may their hearts, repenting,
'Seek for aid in future years.
'Wisdom scorned knows no relenting
'Virtue is not won by tears.

'Fain would we your steps reclaim
30   'Waken fear and holy shame
'And to this end, our council well
'And kindly doomed you to a cell
'Whose darkness, may perchance, disclose
'A beacon-guide from sterner woes –'

So spake my judge – then seized his lamp
And left me in the dungeon damp.
A vault-like place whose stagnant air
Suggests and nourishes despair!

Rosina, this had never been
40   Except for you, my despot queen!
Except for you the billowy sea
Would now be tossing under me
The winds' wild voice my bosom thrill
And my glad heart bound wilder still

Flying before the rapid gale
Those wondrous southern isles to hail
Which wait for my companions free
But thank your passion – not for me!

You know too well – and so do I
50   Your haughty beauty's sovereignty
Yet I have read those falcon eyes –
Have dived into their mysteries –
Have studied long their glance and feel
It is not love those eyes reveal –

They flash they burn with lightening shine
But not with such fond fire as mine;
The tender star fades faint and wan
Before Ambition's scorching sun –
So deem I how – and Time will prove
60   If I have wronged Rosina's love –

Nov. 11th 1844.

32   *Dec 2d. 1844.*
From a D.W. in the N.C. A.G.A.

'O Day, he cannot die
'When thou so fair art shining.
'O sun in such a glorious sky
'So tranquilly declining,

'He cannot leave thee now
'While fresh west winds are blowing
'And all around his youthful brow
'Thy cheerful light is glowing!

'Elbë awake, awake!
10   'The golden evening gleams
'Warm and bright on Arden's lake
'Arouse thee from thy dreams!

'Beside thee, on my knee

'My dearest friend, I pray
'That thou – to cross the eternal sea
'Wouldst yet <u>one</u> hour delay!

'I hear its billows roar
'I see them foaming high
'But no glimpse of a further shore
20   'Has blessed my straining eye –

'Believe not what they urge
'Of Eden isles beyond
'Turn back, from that tempestuous surge
'To thy (own) native land!

'It is not Death, but pain
'That struggles in thy breast;
'(Nay), rally, (Elbë), rouse again
'I cannot let thee rest!'

One long look that sore reproved me
30   For the woe I could not bear –
One mute look of suffering moved me
To repent my useless prayer;

And with sudden check the heaving
Of distraction passed away;
Not a sign of further grieving
Stirred my soul that awful day

Paled at length, that sweet sun setting
Sank to peace the gentle breeze
Summer dews fell softly wetting
40   Glen and glade and silent trees

Then his eyes began to weary
Weighed beneath a (mortal) sleep
And their light grew strangely dreary –
Clouded, even as they would weep –

But they wept not, but they changed not –
Never moved and never closed –
Troubled still and still they ranged not
Wandered not nor yet reposed!

So I knew that he was dying,
50   Stooped and raised his languid head –
Felt no breath and heard no sighing –
So, I knew that he was dead –

Sept. 1826

33 D.G.C. to J.A.

Come, the wind may never again
Blow as now it blows for us
And the stars may never again, shine as now, they shine:
Long before October returns
Seas of blood will have parted us
And you must crush the love in your heart
And I, the love in mine!

For face to face will our kindred stand
And as they are so we shall be
10   Forgetting how the same sweet earth has borne and nourished all –
One must fight for the people's power
And one for the rights of Royalty
And each be ready to give his life to work the other's fall –

The chance of war we cannot shun
Nor would we shrink from our father's cause
Nor dread Death more because the hand that gives it may be dear
We must bear to see Ambition rule
Over Love, with his iron laws;
Must yield our blood for a stranger's sake and refuse ourselves a tear!

20   So, the wind may never again
Blow as now it blows for us
And the stars may never again shine as now they shine
Next October, the cannon's roar
From hostile ranks may be urging us –
Me to strike for your life's blood and you to strike for mine –

October 2d 1844.

34 *I.M. to I.G.*

'The winter wind is loud and wild
'Come close to me my darling child!
'Forsake thy books and mateless play
'And while the night is closing grey,
'We'll talk its pensive hours away –

' Iernë, round our sheltered hall
'November's blasts unheeded call
'Not one fair breath can enter here
'Enough to wave my daughter's hair.

10   'And I am glad to watch the blaze
'Glance from her eyes with mimic rays:
'To feel her cheek so softly pressed
'In happy quiet on my breast;

'But yet, even this tranquillity
'Brings bitter, restless thoughts to me
'And in the red fire's cheerful glow
'I think of deep glens blocked with snow

'I dream of moor and misty hill
'Where evening gathers dark and chill,
20   'For, lone among the mountains cold
'Lie those that I have loved of old
'And my heart aches in speechless pain
'Exhausted with repinings vain
'That I shall see them ne'er again!'

'Father, in early infancy
'When you were far beyond the sea
'Such thoughts were tyrants over me –
'I often sat for hours together
'Through the long nights of angry weather
30   'Raised on my pillow, to descry
'The dim moon struggling in the sky
'Or with strained ear to catch the shock
'Of rock with wave and wave with rock;
'So would I fearful vigil keep
'And, all for listening, never sleep;
'But this world's life has much to dread
'Not so, my Father with the Dead.

'O, not for them should we despair
'The grave is drear but they are not there;
40   'Their dust is mingled with the sod.

'Their happy souls are gone to God!
'You told me this, and yet you sigh
'And murmur that your friends must die
'Ah my dear father, tell me why?

'For if your former words were true
'How useless would such sorrow be!
'As wise to mourn the seed which grew
'Unnoticed on its parent tree

'Because it fell in fertile earth
50 'And sprang up to a glorious birth –
'Struck deep its roots and lifted high
'Its green boughs in the breezy sky!

'But I'll not fear – I will not weep
'For those whose bodies lie asleep:
'I know there is a blessed shore
'Opening its ports for me and mine
'And, gazing Time's wide waters o'er
'I weary for that land divine

'Where we were born – where you and I
60 'Shall meet our Dearest, when we die:
'From suffering and corruption free
'Restored into the Deity.'

Well hast thou spoken, sweet, trustful child!
And wiser than thy sire;
And coming tempests, raging wild,
Shall strengthen thy desire –

Thy fervent hope, through storm and foam,
Through wind and ocean's roar
To reach at last, the eternal home –
70 The steadfast, changeless shore! –

November 6th. 1844

35 *M. Douglas to E. R. Gleneden*

The moon is full this winter night;
The stars are clear, though few
And every window glistens bright
With leaves of frozen dew –

The sweet moon through your lattice gleams
And lights your room like day
And, there, you pass in happy dreams
The peaceful hours away;

While I, with effort hardly quelling
10   The anguish in my breast
Wander about the silent dwelling
And cannot think of rest.

The old clock in the gloomy hall
Ticks on from hour to hour
And every time, its measured call
Seems lingering slow and slower.

And O how slow that keen-eyed star
Has tracked the chilly grey!
What watching yet, how very far
20   The morning lies away!

Beside your chamber door I stand
Love, are you slumbering still?
My cold heart underneath my hand
Has almost ceased to thrill

Bleak, bleak the east wind sobs and sighs
And drowns the turret bell
Whose sad note undistinguished, dies
Unheard, like my farewell –

Tomorrow Scorn will blight my name
30   And Hate will trample me –
Will load me with a coward's shame
A Traitor's perjury!

False Friends will launch their venomed sneers.
True Friends will wish me dead;
And I shall cause the bitterest tears
That you have ever shed!

The dark deeds of my outlawed race
Will then like virtues shine;
And men will pardon their disgrace
40   Beside the guilt of mine;

For who forgives the accursed crime
Of dastard treachery?
Rebellion in its chosen time
May Freedom's champion be –

Revenge may stain a righteous sword
It may be just to slay;
But, Traitor, Traitor. From that word
All true breasts shrink away!

O, I would give my heart to death
50   To keep my Honour Fair
Yet I'll not give my inward Faith
My Honour's name to spare.

Not even to keep your priceless love
Dare I, Beloved, deceive;
This treason should the Future prove
Gleneden, then believe!

I know the path I ought to go,
I follow fearlessly;
Enquiring not what deeper woe
60   Stern Duty stores for me –

So, Foes pursue, and cold allies
Mistrust me, every one;
Let me be false in others' eyes
If faithful in my own –

November 21st 1844

36 *R Alcona to J Brenzaida*

Cold in the earth and the deep snow piled above thee!
Far, far removed   cold in the dreary grave!
Have I forgot, my Only Love to love thee,
Severed at last by Time's allwearing wave?

Now, when alone, do my thoughts no longer hover
Over the mountains on Angora's shore:
Resting their wings where heath and fern-leaves cover
That noble heart for ever, ever more?

Cold in the earth, and fifteen wild Decembers
10 From those brown hills have melted into spring –
Faithful indeed is the spirit that remembers
After such years of change and suffering!

Sweet Love of youth, forgive if I forget thee
While the world's tide is bearing me along
Sterner desires and darker Hopes beset me
Hopes which obscure but cannot do thee wrong –

No other sun has lightened up my heaven:
No other star has ever shone for me
All my life's bliss from thy dear life was given –
20 All my life's bliss is in the grave with thee!

But when the days of golden dreams had perished
And even Despair was powerless to destroy
Then did I learn how existence could be cherished
Strengthened and fed – without the aid of joy

Then did I check the tears of useless passion,
Weaned my young soul from yearning after thine;
Sternly denied its burning wish to hasten
Down to that tomb already more than mine!

And even yet, I dare not let it languish,
30 Dare not indulge in Memory's rapturous pain!
Once drinking deep of that divinest anguish
How could I seek the empty world again?

March 3d. 1845

37 *H.A. and A.S.*

In the same place, where Nature wore
The same celestial glow,
I'm sure I've seen these forms before
But many springs ago;

And only <u>he</u> had locks of light
And <u>she</u> had raven hair;
While now, his curls are dark as night,
And hers, as morning, fair.

Besides, I've dreamt of tears whose traces
10   Will never more depart,
Of agony that fast effaces
The verdure of the heart.

I dreamt, one sunny day like this,
In this peerless month of May
I saw her give the unanswered kiss
As his spirit passed away:

Those young eyes that so sweetly shine
Then looked their last adieu
And pale Death changed that cheek divine
20   To his unchanging hue

And earth was cast above the breast
That beats so warm and free
Where her soft ringlets lightly rest
And move responsively.

Then she, upon the covered grave –
The grass grown grave, did lie.
A tomb not girt by Gondal's wave
Nor arched by Gondal's sky.

The sod was sparkling bright with dew
30   But brighter still with tears
That welled from mortal grief, I knew
Which never heals with years –

And if he came not for her woe
He would not now return;
He would not leave his sleep below
When she had ceased to mourn –

O Innocence, that cannot live
With heart-wrung anguish long
Dear childhood's Innocence, forgive,
40   For I have done thee wrong!

The bright rosebuds, those hawthorns shroud
Within their perfumed bower –
Have never closed beneath a cloud,
Nor bent before a shower –

Had darkness once obscured their sun
Or kind dew turned to rain
No storm cleared sky that ever shone
Could win such bliss again –

May 17th 1842.

38 *Rodric Lesley. 1830*

Lie down and rest – the fight is done.
Thy comrades to the camp retire;
Gaze not so earnestly upon
The far gleam of the beacon fire.

Listen not to the wind-borne sounds
Of music and of soldiers' cheer:
Thou canst not go – unnumbered wounds
Exhaust thy life and hold thee here –

Had that hand power to raise the sword
10   Which since this morn laid hundreds low
Had that tongue strength to speak the word
That urged thy followers on the foe

Were that warm blood within thy veins
Which now upon the earth is flowing
Splashing its sod with crimson stains
Reddening the pale heath round thee growing

Then Rodric, thou mightst still be turning
With eager eye and anxious breast
To where those signal lights are burning –
20   To where thy monarch's legions rest.

But never more – look up and see
The twilight fading from the skies

That last dim beam that sets for thee,
Rodric, for thee shall never rise!

Dec 18th 1843.

39

A thousand sounds of happiness
And only one of real distress:
One hardly uttered groan –
But that has hushed all vocal joy,
Eclipsed the glory of the sky
And made me think that misery
Rules in our world alone!

About his face the sunshine glows
And in his hair the south wind blows
10 And violet and wild woodrose
Are sweetly breathing near

Nothing without suggests dismay
If he could force his mind away
From tracking farther day by day
The desert of Despair –

Too truly agonized to weep
His eyes are motionless as sleep,
His frequent sighs longdrawn and deep
Are anguish to my ear
20 And I would soothe – but can I call
The cold corpse from its funeral pall
And cause a gleam of hope to fall
With my consoling tear?

O, Death, so many spirits driven
Through this false world, their all had given
To win the everlasting haven
To sufferers so divine –
Why didst thou smite the loved the blest
The ardent and the happy breast
30 That full of hope desired not rest
And shrank appalled from thine?

At least, since thou will not restore
In mercy launch one arrow more
Life's concious Death it wearies sore
It tortures worse than thee –
Enough of storms have bowed his head,
Grant him at last a quiet bed
Beside his early stricken Dead –
Even where he yearns to be!

April 22d 1845

40 *A.E. and R.C.*

Heavy hangs the raindrop
From the burdened spray;
Heavy broods the damp mist
On Uplands far away;

Heavy looms the dull sky.
Heavy rolls the sea –
And heavy beats the young heart
Beneath that lonely tree –

Never has a blue streak
10   Cleft the clouds since morn –
Never has his grim Fate
Smiled since he was born –

Frowning on the infant,
Shadowing childhood's joy;
Guardian angel knows not
That melancholy boy.

Day is passing swiftly
Its sad and sombre prime:
Youth is fast invading
20   Sterner manhood's time –

All the flowers are praying
For sun before they close
And he prays too, unknowing.
That sunless human rose!

Blossoms, that the west wind
Has never wooed to blow

Scentless are your petals,
Your dew as cold as snow.

Soul, where kindred kindness
30   No early promise woke
Barren is your beauty
As weed upon the rock –

Wither, Brother, wither,
You were vainly given –
Earth reserves no blessing
For the unblessed of Heaven!

Child of Delight! with sunbright hair,
And seablue, seadeep eyes
Spirit of Bliss, what brings thee here,
40   Beneath these sullen skies?

Thou shouldest live in eternal spring
Where endless day is never dim
Why, seraph, has thy erring wing
Borne thee down to weep with him?

'Ah, not from heaven am I descended
'And I do not come to mingle tears
'But sweet is day though with shadows blended
'And though clouded, sweet are youthful years –

'I, the image of light and gladness
50   'Saw and pitied that mournful boy,
'I swore to take his gloomy sadness
'And give to him my beamy joy –

'Heavy and dark the night is closing
'Heavy and dark may its biding be
'Better for all from grief reposing,
'And better for all who watch like me –

'Guardian angel, he lacks no longer;
'Evil fortune he need not fear:
'Fate is strong but Love is stronger
60   'And more unsleeping than angel's care.'

May 28th 1845.

41 *M.A.   Written on the Dungeon Wall. N C*

I know that tonight, the wind is sighing
The soft August wind, over forest and moor
While I in a grave-like chill am lying
On the damp black flags of my dungeon-floor –

I know that the Harvest moon is shining;
She neither will wax nor wane for me.
Yet I weary, weary, with vain repining,
One gleam of her heaven-bright face to see!

For this constant darkness is wasting the gladness
10   Fast wasting the gladness of life away:
It gathers up thoughts akin to madness
That never would cloud the world of day –

I chide with my soul – I bid it cherish
The feelings it lived on when I was free,
But, shrinking it murmurs, 'Let Memory perish
Forget for thy Friends have forgotten thee!'

Alas, I did think that they were weeping
Such tears as I weep – it is not so!
Their careless young eyes are closed in sleeping
20   Their brows are unshadowed, undimmed by woe –

Might I go to their beds, I'd rouse that slumber,
My spirit should startle their rest and tell
How hour after hour, I wakefully number
Deep buried from light in my lonely cell!

Yet let them dream on, though dreary dreaming
Would haunt my pillow if they were here
And I were laid warmly under the gleaming
Of that guardian moon and her comrade star –

Better that I my own fate mourning
30   Should pine alone in the prison-gloom
Than waken free on the summer morning
And feel they were suffering this awful doom.

M A

August 1845

42 *Julian M. and A. G. Rochelle*

Silent is the House – all are laid asleep:
One, alone, looks out o'er the snow-wreaths deep;
Watching every cloud, dreading every breeze
That whirls the wildering drifts and bends the groaning trees –

Cheerful is the hearth, soft the matted floor
Not one shivering gust creeps through pane or door
The little lamp burns straight; its rays shoot strong and far
I trim it well to be the Wanderer's guiding-star –

Frown my haughty Sire, chide, my angry Dame;
Set your slaves to spy, threaten me with shame;
But neither Sire nor dame, nor prying serf shall know
What angel nightly tracks that waste of winter snow –

In the dungeon crypts idly did I stray
Reckless of the lives wasting there away;
'Draw the ponderous bars, open Warder stern!'
He dare not say me nay. The hinges harshly turn.

'Our guests are darkly lodged' I whispered gazing through
The vault whose grated eye showed heaven more grey than blue;
(This was when glad spring laughed in awaking pride)
'Aye, darkly lodged enough!' returned my sullen guide.

Then, God forgive my youth, forgive my careless tongue!
I scoffed as the chill chains on the damp flagstones rung;
'Confined in triple walls, art thou so much to fear.
'That we must bind thee down and clench thy fetters here?'

The captive raised her face, it was as soft and mild
As sculptured marble saint or slumbering, unweaned child.
It was so soft and mild, it was so sweet and fair
Pain could not trace a line nor grief a shadow there!

The captive raised her hand and pressed it to her brow
'I have been struck', she said, 'and I am suffering now
'Yet these are little worth, your bolts and irons strong
'And were they forged in steel they could not hold me long' –

Hoarse laughed the jailor grim, 'Shall I be won to hear
'Dost think fond, dreaming wretch that I shall grant thy prayer?
'Or better still, wilt melt my master's heart with groans?
'Ah sooner might the sun thaw down these granite stones! –

'My master's voice is low, his aspect bland and kind
'But hard as hardest flint the soul that lurks behind:
'And I am rough and rude, yet, not more rough to see
40   'Than is the hidden ghost which has its home in me!'

About her lips there played a smile of almost scorn
'My friend', she gently said, 'you have not heard me mourn
'When you, my parent's lives – my lost life can restore
'Then I may weep and sue, but never, Friend, before!'

Her head sank on her hands its fair curls swept the ground
The Dungeon seemed to swim in strange confusion round –
'Is she so near to death?' I murmured, half aloud
And kneeling, parted back the floating golden cloud

Alas, how former days upon my heart were borne
50   How memory mirrored then the prisoner's joyous morn.
Too blithe, too loving child, too warmly, wildly gay!
Was that the wintry close of thy celestial May?

She knew me and she sighed 'Lord Julian, can it be,
'Of all my playmates, you, alone, remember me?
'Nay start not at my words, unless you deem it shame
'To own from conquered foe, a once familiar name –

'I can not wonder now at ought the world will do
'And insult and contempt I lightly brook from you,
'Since those who vowed away their souls to win my love
60   'Around this living grave like utter strangers move:

'Nor has one voice been raised to plead that I might die
'Not buried under earth but in the open sky;
'By ball or speedy knife or headsman's skillful blow
'A quick and welcome pang instead of lingering woe!

'Yet, tell them, Julian, all, I am not doomed to wear
'Year after year in gloom and desolate despair;
'A messenger of Hope comes every night to me,
'And offers, for short life, eternal liberty –

'He comes with western winds, with evening's wandering airs,
70   'With that clear dusk of heaven that brings the thickest stars;
'Winds take a pensive tone and stars a tender fire
'And visions rise and change which kill me with desire –

'Desire for nothing known in my maturer years
'When joy grew mad with awe at counting future tears:

'When, if my spirit's sky, was full of flashes warm,
'I knew not whence they came from sun or thunderstorm:

'But first a hush of peace, a soundless calm descends;
'The struggle of distress and fierce impatience ends;
'Mute music soothes my breast – unuttered harmony
80   'That I could never dream till earth was lost to me.

'Then dawns the Invisible, the Unseen its truth reveals;
'My outward sense is gone, my inward essence feels –
'Its wings are almost free, its home, its harbour found;
'Measuring the gulf it stoops and dares the final bound! –

O, dreadful is the check – intense the agony
When the ear begins to hear and the eye begins to see,
When the pulse begins to throb, the brain to think again,
The soul to feel the flesh and the flesh to feel the chain!

'Yet I would lose no sting, would wish no torture less;
90   'The more that anguish racks the earlier it will bless:
'And robed in fires of Hell, or bright with heavenly shine
'If it but herald Death, the vision is divine – '

She ceased to speak, and I, unanswering, watched her there
Not daring now to touch one lock of silken hair –
As I had knelt in scorn, on the dank floor I knelt still,
My fingers in the links of that iron hard and chill –

I heard and yet heard not the surly Keeper growl;
I saw, yet did not see, the flagstones damp and foul:
The Keeper, to and fro, paced by the bolted door
100   And shivered as he walked and as he shivered, swore –

While my cheek glowed in flame, I marked that he did rave
Of air that froze his blood and moisture like the grave –
'We have been two hours good!' he muttered peevishly,
Then, loosing off his belt the rusty dungeon key,

He said, 'You may be pleased, Lord Julian, still to stay
'But duty will not let me linger here all day:
'If I might go, I'd leave this badge of mine with you
'Not doubting that you'd prove a jailor stern and true'

I took the proffered charge; the captive's drooping lid
110   Beneath its shady lash a sudden lightening hid
Earth's hope was not so dead heaven's home was not so dear;
I read it in that flash of longing quelled by fear

Then like a tender child whose hand did just enfold
Safe in its eager grasp a bird it wept to hold
When pierced with one wild glance from the troubled hazel eye
It gushes into tears and lets its treasure fly

Thus ruth and selfish love together striving tore
The heart all newly taught to pity and adore;
If I should break the chain I felt my bird would go
120   Yet I must break the chain or seal the prisoner's woe –.

Short strife what rest could soothe – What peace could visit me
While she lay pining there for Death to set her free?
'Rochelle, the dungeons teem with foes to gorge our hate –
'Thou art too young to die by such a bitter fate!'

With hurried blow on blow I struck the fetters through
Regardless how that deed, my after hours might rue
Oh, I was over-blest by the warm unasked embrace –
By the smile of grateful joy that lit her angel face!

And I was overblest – aye, more than I could dream
130   When, faint, she turned aside from noon's unwonted beam,
When though the cage was wide – the heaven around it lay –
Its pinion would not waft my wounded dove away –

Through thirteen anxious weeks of terror-blent delight
I guarded her by day and guarded her by night
While foes were prowling near and Death gazed greedily
And only Hope remained a faithful friend to me –

Then oft with taunting smile, I heard my kindred tell
'How Julian loved his hearth and sheltering rooftree well, –
How the trumpet's voice might call the battle standard wave
140   But Julian had no heart to fill a patriot's grave – '

And I, who am so quick to answer sneer with sneer:
So ready to condemn to scorn a coward's fear –
I held my peace like one whose conscience keeps him dumb
And saw my kinsman go – and lingered still at home.

Another hand than mine, my rightful banner held
And gathered my renown on Freedom's crimson field
Yet I had no desire the glorious prize to gain –
It needed braver nerve to face the world's disdain –

And by the patient strength that could that world defy;
150 By suffering, with calm mind, contempt and calumny;
By never-doubting love, unswerving constancy,
Rochelle, I earned at last an equal love from thee!

October 9th 1845

43

Why ask to know the date – the clime?
More than mere words they cannot be:
Men knelt to God and worshipped crime,
And crushed the helpless, even as we.

But they had learnt from length of strife –
Of civil war and anarchy,
To laugh at death and look on life
With somewhat lighter sympathy.

It was the autumn of the year;
10 The time to labouring peasants, dear,
And, week after week, from noon to noon,
September shone as bright as June –
Still, never hand a sickle held;
The crops were garnered in the field –
Trod out, and ground by horses' feet
While every ear was milky sweet;
And kneaded on the threshing-floor
With mire of tears and human gore.
Some said, they thought that heaven's pure rain
20 Would hardly bless those fields again.
Not so – the all-benignant skies
Rebuked that fear of famished eyes –
July passed on with showers and dew,
And August glowed in showerless blue;
No harvest time could be more fair
Had harvest fruits but ripened there.

And I confess that hate of rest,
And thirst for things abandoned now,
Has weaned me from my country's breast
30 And brought me to that land of woe.

Enthusiast – in a name delighting,
My alien sword I drew to free
One race, beneath two standards fighting,
For loyalty, and liberty –

When kindred strive, God help the weak!
A brother's ruth 'tis vain to seek:
At first, it hurt my chivalry
To join them in their cruelty;
But I grew hard – I learnt to wear
40   An iron front to terror's prayer;
I learnt to turn my ears away
From torture's groans, as well as they.
By force I learnt – what power had I
To say the conquered should not die?
What heart, one trembling foe to save
When hundreds daily filled the grave?
Yet, there <u>were</u> faces that could move
A moment's flash of human love;
And there were fates that made me feel
50   I was not to the centre, steel –

I've often witnessed wise men fear
To meet distress which they foresaw;
And seeming cowards nobly bear
A doom that thrilled the brave with awe:

Strange proofs I've seen, how hearts could hide
Their secret with a life-long pride,
And then, reveal it as they died –
Strange courage, and strange weakness too,
In that last hour when most are true,
60   And timid natures strangely nerved
To deeds from which the desperate swerved
These (I) may tell, but leave them now.
Go with me where my thoughts would go;
How all to-day, and all last night
I've had one scene before my sight –

Wood-shadowed dales, a harvest moon
Unclouded in its glorious noon;
A solemn landscape wide and still;
A red fire on a distant hill –
70   A line of fires, and deep below,
Another duskier, drearier glow –
Charred beams, and lime, and blackened stones
Self-piled in cairns o'er burning bones
And lurid flames that licked the wood

Then quenched their glare in pools of blood –
But yestereve – No! never care;
Let street and suburb smoulder there –
Smoke-hidden, in the winding glen,
They lay too far to vex my ken.

80   Four score shot down – all veterans strong –
One prisoner spared, their leader young –
And he within his house was laid,
Wounded, and weak and nearly dead.
We gave him life against his will;
For he entreated us to kill –
But statue-like we saw his tears –
And harshly fell our captain's sneers!

'Now, heaven forbid!' with scorn he said.
'That noble gore our hands should shed
90   Like common blood – retain thy breath
Or scheme, if thou canst purchase death –
When men are poor we sometimes hear
And pitying grant that dastard prayer;
When men are rich we make them buy
The pleasant privilege, to die –
O, we have castles reared for kings
Embattled towers and buttressed wings.
Thrice three feet thick, and guarded well
With chain, and bolt, and sentinel!
100   We build our despots' dwellings sure;
Knowing they love to live secure –
And our respect for royalty
Extends to thy estate and thee!'

The suppliant groaned, his moistened eye
Swam wild and dim with agony.
The gentle blood could ill sustain
Degrading taunts, unhonoured pain.
Bold had he shown himself to lead;
Eager to smite and proud to bleed –
110   A man amid the battle's storm;
An infant in the after calm.

Beyond the town his mansion stood
Girt round with pasture-land and wood;
And there our wounded soldiers lying
Enjoyed the ease of wealth in dying:

For him, no mortal more than he
Had softened life with luxury;

And truly did our priest declare
'Of good things he had had his share.'

120   We lodged him in an empty place
The full moon beaming on his face
Through shivered glass, and ruins, made
Where shell and ball the fiercest played –
I watched his ghastly couch beside
Regardless if he lived or died –
Nay, muttering curses on the breast
Whose ceaseless moans denied me rest:

'Twas hard, I know, 'twas harsh to say
'Hell snatch thy worhless soul away!'
130   But then 'twas hard my lids to keep,
Night following night estranged from sleep.
Captive and keeper, both outworn,
Each in his misery yearned for morn;
Even though returning morn should bring
Intenser toil and suffering.

Slow, slow it came! Our dreary room
Grew drearier with departing gloom;
Yet, as the (urgent) wind warmly blew
I felt my pulses bound anew,
140   And turned to him – nor breeze, nor ray
Revived that mould of shattered clay,
Scarce conscious of his pain he lay –
Scarce conscious that my hands removed
The glittering toys his lightness loved;
The jewelled rings, and locket fair
Where rival curls of silken hair,
Sable and brown revealed to me
A tale of doubtful constancy.

'Forsake the world without regret,'
150   I murmured in contemptuous tone;
The world, poor wretch, will soon forget
Thy noble name when thou art gone!
Happy, if years of slothful shame
Could perish like a noble name – !
If God did no account require
And being with breathing might expire!'
And words of (such contempt) I said
Cold insults o'er a dying bed
Which as they darken memory now
160   Disturb my pulse and flush my brow:
I know what justice holds in store,

Reprisals for those days of gore
Not for blood spilt, but for the sin
Of stifling mercy's voice within.
The blood spilt gives no pang at all;
It is my conscience haunting me,
Telling how oft my lips shed gall
On many a thing too weak to be,
Even in thought,   [. . .]
170 And whispering ever, when I pray,
'God will repay – God will repay!'
He does repay and soon and well
The deeds that turn his earth to hell,
The wrongs that aim a venomed dart
Through nature at the Eternal Heart,
Surely my cruel tongue was cursed
I know my prisoner heard me speak
A transient gleam of feeling burst
And wandered o'er his haggard cheek
180 And from his quivering lids there stole
A look to melt a daemon's soul
A silent prayer more powerful far
Than any breathed petitions are
Pleading in mortal agony
To mercy's Source but not to me –
Now I recall that glance and groan
And wring my hands in vain distress
Then I was adamantine stone
Nor felt one touch of tenderness.
190 My plunder ta'en I left him there
Without a [. . .] of morning air
To struggle with his last despair
Regardless of the 'wild(ered) cry
Which wailed for death, yet wailed to die
I left him there unwatched alone
And eager sought the court below
Where o'er a trough of chiselled stone
An ice cold well did gurgling flow
The water in its basin shed
200 A stronger tinge of   ?gory red
I drank and scarcely marked the hue
My food was dyed with crimson too
As I went out, a ?wizzened child
With wasted cheek and ringlets wild
A shape of fear and misery
Raised up her [. . .] hands to me
And begged her father's (face) to see
I spurned the piteous wretch away
Thy father's face is lifeless clay

210 As thine may'st be ere fall of day
Unless the truth be quickly told
Where they have hid thy father's gold

Yet in the intervals of pain
He heard my taunts and moaned again
And mocking moans I did reply
And asked him why he would not die
In noble silent (agony) – uncomplaining
Was it not foul disgrace and shame
To thus disgrace his ancient name
220 Just then a comrade came hurrying in
Alas he cried sin gender(s) sin.
For every soldier slain they've sworn
To hang up five tomorrow morn
They've ta'en of stranglers sixty-three
Full thirty from one company
And all my father's family
And comrade thou hadst only one
They've ta'en thy all, thy little son
Down at my captives feet I fell
230 I had no option in despair
As thou wouldst save thy soul from hell
My own heart's darling bid them spare
Or human hate and hate divine
Blight every orphan flower of thine
(He) raised his head from death beguiled,
He wakened up he almost smiled
I lost last night my only child
Twice in my arms twice on my knee
You stabbed my child and laughed at me
240 And so with choking voice he said
I trust in God I hope she's dead
Yet not to thee, not even to thee
Would I return such misery
Death brought that fearful grief I know
I will not cause thee equal woe
{Write that they kill
{Write that they harm no infant there
Write that it is my latest prayer
I wrote he signed and thus did save
My treasure from the gory grave
250 And O my [. . .] longed wildly then
To give his saviour life again
And he would face a [. . .] godly man
And then I felt an
Have given his saviour life again

But heedless of my gratitude
The silent corpse before me lay
And still methinks in gloomy mood
I see it fresh as yesterday
The sad face raised imploringly
260   To mercy's God and not to me
And mercy's God [. . .]
The last [. . .] of [. . .] House
I could not rescue him his child
I found alive, and tended well
But she was [. . .] anguish wild
And hated [. . .] like [. . .] hell
And weary with her (savage) woe
One moonless night I let her go

14 September 1846

44

Why ask to know what date, what clime
There dwelt our own humanity
Power-worshippers from earliest time
Foot-kissers of trimphant crime
Crushers of helpless misery
Crushing down justice honouring wrong
If that be feeble this be strong
Shedders of blood shedders of tears
Self- [. . .] avid of distress
10   Yet mocking heaven with senseless prayers
For mercy on the merciless.

It was the autumn of the year
When grain grows yellow in the ear
Day after day, from noon to noon
The August sun blazed bright as June
{[. . .] with heedless unregarding eyes
{But we more careless of the skies
Saw panting earth and glowing skies
No hand the reaper's sickle held
Nor bound the ripe sheaves in the field
20   Our corn was garnered months before
Threshed out [. . .] kneaded-up with gore
Ground when the [. . .] were milky sweet
With furious toil [. . .] and feet
I, doubly cursed [. . .] foreign sod
Fought neither for my home nor God

May 13th 1848

Notes

Explanations to the Notes

Sources

There are three sources to be tapped for Emily Brontë's poems:

1. The manuscripts. The notebooks into which Emily Brontë copied up her poems:
    (a) The Ashley MS, a notebook containing poems written between July 1837 and October 1839: in the British Library.
    (b) Gondal Poems – in the British Library.
    (c) E.J.B. – the whereabouts of this manuscript is not known. There is a facsimile of it in the *Shakespeare Head Brontë* edition.
    (d) Separate, often isolated, pages of earlier versions of the poems before they were copied into the later notebooks – many of these are in the library at Haworth.
    The poems in this edition are from a, b, and c.

2. The published editions:
    (a) 1846 – in which Emily had a hand.
    (b) 1850 – Charlotte's edition of *Wuthering Heights and Agnes Grey*, with additional poems by Ellis and Acton Bell. Charlotte altered words, phrases and added lines.

3. Two transcriptions by Charlotte's husband, the Rev. A. B. Nicholls, of poems not printed in 1846 or 1850, one in the Huntingdon Library, the other in the New York Public Library, U.S.A. The poems transcribed are the same in both. The Huntingdon copy has been used here for reference where there are difficulties in deciphering Emily's script.

The Notes

There are three sections in the Notes:

a   the additions/alterations on the notebook manuscripts
b   variations in earlier version(s) of the poem
c   variations printed in either the 1846 or the 1850 volumes.

All three sections are dealt with in the Notes to each poem, though sections are omitted where there is nothing to record i.e. no alterations on the MS, or no earlier or later version of the poem.

There are other marks on the manuscripts, such as asterisks or *Pubd.* or occasionally a drawing of a hand with a finger pointing to the first line (where a poem was chosen for publication); where A. B. Nicholls has chosen a poem for transcription, it is marked with his initials and sometimes a circle; lines extracted for publication may be marked by a line down the left-hand margin. These markings are not recorded.

a   *Alterations*

Key to references in the notes
1. The alterations can be written in either long hand = l/h
or print hand = p/h
2. Words/phrases written between lines = interlined
3. Crossings-out
    (i)   words/phrases crossed through but what is underneath still legible:
           e.g. *yet* crossed through: *but* above/underneath/at the side/in margin
    (ii)   when what is underneath is illegible:
           e.g. illeg. crossed through: *but* above/underneath/etc
    (iii) when both what is underneath and the replacement are illegible:
           e.g. illeg. crossed through: illeg. above/underneath/etc.
4. Over-writing
    (i)   when new word simply written on top of the original:
           e.g. *yet* overwritten by *but*
    (ii)   when impossible to decide which is the original which the alternative:
           e.g. yet/but
    (iii) when it is impossible to decide which of two words it is:
           e.g. thy = my (these two are often very difficult to differentiate)
5. Illegible words/phrases
    (i)   ?xxxx
    (ii)   in the text – where an illegible word/phrase has been taken from another source (e.g. the 1846, 1850 volumes) brackets are used; where there is no other source except that of subsequent editors, rather than accept an interpretation that often seems to be based more on luck than good judgement (particularly Gon 43, 44) I have left spaces in the text.
6. Charlotte's alterations
    (i)   when the same word is written above or at the side in longhand, it is usually a clarification of E.'s writing by C.
           (for C.'s pencil alterations on the Gondal MS see note to the manuscript in the BL Catalogue.)
    (ii)   variations written on the MS identical with those printed in her 1850 edition.

b *and* c

Earlier and later versions are given in the Notes to each poem, with the Notebook MS version in brackets.

For spelling and punctuation see p.184.

The poems are not numbered in the Notebooks. The numbers given here follow the order in which the poems are copied into the books.

Abbreviations

Ash   = Ashley Notebook
BPM = Brontë Parsonage Museum
Bonn = Bonnell Collection in the Brontë Parsonage Museum
EJB   = notebook headed 'E.J.B., Transcribed February 1844', facsimile in
        SHB.
Gon   = notebook headed 'Emily Jane Brontë Transcribed February 1844'
Howe = MSS in the Howe Collections, New York Public Library
SHB   = *Shakespeare Head Brontë* ed T. J. Wise and J. A. Symington, 19 volumes,
        1931–8; reprinted Basil Blackwell 1980
BL   = British Library
E.   = Emily Brontë
C.   = Charlotte Brontë
A.   = Anne Brontë
B.   = Branwell Brontë
ABN   = Rev. A. B. Nicholls

Ashley MS

This notebook, now in the British Library, contains the sixteen poems Emily chose to transcribe from those she wrote between July 1837 and October 1839. The pages of the notebook itself were taken apart and mounted on guards and rebound by T. J. Wise. Frequently word(s), letter(s) and/or punctuation at the end of a line are cut off by either the mount, or the tightness of the binding. Emily herself seems to have had problems with the narrowness of the pages of the notebook. Often she had to tuck the last word(s) of a line above the end of the line itself to get them in.

The first page(s), as well as those containing lines 4–33 of no. 13, are missing. There was no mention of pages missing in the description of the manuscript when T. J. Wise offered it for sale. Was it intact then or were the missing pages merely ignored? Had the Rev. Nicholls sold the original notebook with pages already torn out? As the other poems in this notebook that Emily later transcribed are cancelled by being crossed through with diagonal lines, it rather suggests that tearing out pages was not Emily's way of cancelling transcribed poems. The lower edges of the pages are either roughly cut or torn.

The notebook is unusual in that it is written in longhand. In their juvenilia, all the Brontës used a minute print script. Originally this was to make their writing seem as near as possible to a real printed page. The other two transcribed Notebooks, as well as poems on single sheets, are in this minute script, which is often difficult to decipher – even Charlotte made mistakes at times (see EJB 2 line 4).

The poems are not entered in chronological order of composition. The latest dated poem is 15 October 1839 (no. 9). For some of the poems there are earlier versions: nos. 1, 3, and 6 are in Bonn, no. 2 is in Howe.

Four of the poems (nos. 1, 5, 7, 13) were transcribed into the Gondal notebook: five others (nos. 2, 3, 4, 6, 12) have Gondal references in either the title or the poem itself; one (no. 10) was transcribed into the EJB Notebook (no. 12). Poems nos. 1, 5, 7, 10, 13 are here printed in full only in the Gondal or EJB sections, where any variations are recorded.

There is no heading to this MS as there is to those of 1844, so we have no terms of reference. That only one (no. 10) of the poems finds its way into the EJB Notebook suggests three possibilities: that Emily used this notebook indiscrimately for both Gondal and EJB poems; that it was basically a Gondal notebook and this poem crept in erroneously; that poems written in personal tones (if Gondal, being spoken or thought by a Gondal character) could be moved over into the non-Gondal collection. If the latter is so, this smudges the line between the two main collections of 1844 and suggests that the poems later transcribed into the EJB MS could originally have been centred on Gondal themes and that the personal tone which marks those poems was not, originally, Emily's but that of a Gondal character. Looking at the definitive headings of the 1844 notebooks, this jumbling up of the poems together as all part of the Gondal saga hardly seems feasible. Compromise suggests that, until 1844, notebooks were used for transcribing any poems – Gondal or non-Gondal – she wished to keep, and that, in 1844, she had a grand sorting out of her poems, allotting them to one or other of the two 1844 notebooks, so acknowledging their difference in kind, and then regrouping them according to subject or theme.

1   See Gon 2

2   ***To a Wreath of Snow by A.G. Almeda***, December 1837
    a   4. ?! after *lies* obscured by binding
    b   Earlier version of last seven lines, cancelled by lines across, in Howe.
        Between this and next poem is written, 'Emily Jane Brontë December
        1837': this could apply to poem 2 or poem 3 as, from 4 onwards, the
        dating has been changed from the end to the beginning of the poem.

3   ***Song by Julius Angora***, December 1837
    a   12. *neath* of *beneath* obscured by binding
    b   Earlier cancelled version Bonn dated December 1837, which has no
        differences in the text although fewer punctuation marks in Ash.

5   See Gon 6

6   ***Song to A.A.***, May 1838
    a   Lines 4, 8 spaces arranged thus in MS
    b   Earlier cancelled version in Bonn.
        4. *thou bright haired child* (*my darkhaired child*)
        5. *shivering* (*shuddering*)
        8. *thou fairbrowed child* (*my nursling child*)
        12. *clasps* (*bears*)

7   See Gon 7

8   ***Lines***, December 1837
    a   9. *ere* of *here* obscured by binding
        11. *behind* crossed through: *around* above
           fore of *before* obscured by binding

9   ***Song***, October 15th 1839
    a   4. *while* crossed through: *when* above
        16. *thee* crossed through: *me* above

10   See EJB 12

11   No title, July 26th 1839
    a   18. *shall* crossed through: *will* above
        31. *Compassion: For mercy* alternative above p/h
        32. *Revenge: But hate* alternative above p/h

12   ***A.A.A.*** undated.
    The heading may be *& A.A.* so linking it with the poem before
    a   14. *Helllike* [sic]
        21. *sin* crossed through: *crime* above
           ?tossed/tost obscured by binding

13   See Gon 10

14   ***Lines by Claudia***, May 28th 1839
    a   28. *Thought = Though* [?mis-copied by E.]
        34. *For which we fought and*
                  bled and died

16   *Lines*, April 28th 1839

    a   4. *?nursed/nurtured/nourished: rested* Hatfield

          21. *?A last* smudged through: *Remembrance* above

          24. *sweetly* crossed through: *fondly* above

          44. *?dew* obscured by binding

          45. *within* obscured by binding

          56. *?woe* obscured by binding

Chronological order of poems

1, 15, 2, 3, 8, 5, 6, 10, 13, 4, 16, 7, 14, 11, 12, 9.

EJB Manuscript

According to C. W. Hatfield this MS was in the library of Sir A. J. Law at Honresfield in Lancashire. It carried the bookplate of T. J. Wise and was stamped as being bound for T. J. Wise. The flyleaf was autographed in pencil: 'William Law Littleborough nr. Manchester February 5th 1897'. Hatfield was sent 'photographs of some of the manuscript pages' in 1926. Realizing the inaccuracies of earlier editions, he started his search for the MSS of Emily's poems which culminated in his *Complete Poems of Emily Brontë*, 1941. There have been selections from her poetry since but no complete edition, which undoubtedly bears witness to the care and thoroughness of Hatfield's edition. Since then the original EJB MS has faded from view. However, the *Shakespeare Head Brontë* included in its volumes a facsimile of the complete MS, which, until the reappearance of the Law MS, remains the only source for editorial work.

The MS is a notebook (complementing the Gondal Notebook) containing 31 poems, dated from 5 November 1838 to 2 January 1846. It is in Emily's print hand and all the poems except two (nos. 15, 16) are dated. Its heading is small and modest – just 'E.J.B.' and the date of transcription.

From the entry of poem no. 22, 'My Comforter, February 10th 1844', to the end of the MS the poems are written up in the chronological order* of the dates Emily gives in the heading to each poem. It is from these later poems that the bulk of those selected for the 1846 volume were taken, (nos. 20–30 constitute 11 of the 15 from this notebook).

The first poem in the MS, 'Loud without the wind was roaring', is a celebration of the moors in all the seasons, spoken by an unhappy exile. The lyricism of its rippling rhythms catches the movement and spirit of the wind, of running free on the moors. The MS ends with one of the most assured and consistent poems Emily ever wrote. 'No coward soul is mine' is a clear-eyed, aggressively direct statement of belief. Both are fine examples of Emily's gifts as a poet. It is strange that this last poem, dated 2 January 1846, was not included in the 1846 volume since Charlotte's enquiry about publishing poems was not made until the end of January and the actual MS of the poems by the brothers Bell was not sent to the publishers until February of that year. Did Emily or Charlotte reject it when selecting for the 1846 volume? If so why? Did it express too pagan a creed for a daughter of the manse? Charlotte herself published it, four years later (though it is not as she declares the last poem her sister wrote, it is however the last poem in a complete and finished form) in her 1850 edition of her sisters' novels.

The fact that, in the 1846 volume, 15 poems are from this MS and only six from the Gondal Notebook makes one conjecture that it was this notebook that Charlotte lighted upon in 1845. This may well explain Emily's great anger and, again conjecturing, if it had been the Gondal Notebook Charlotte nosed into, resulting in Emily's days of anger, would Emily have ever readily relinquished the more privately headed, EJB Notebook?

*There is a slight hiccup with no. 23 (April 1843) which seems to have found a place at that point because its theme is common to that of nos. 22, 24, 25 and 26.

1   November 11th 1838
    b   First 10 lines only in Howe.
    c   1850 *Stanzas*
        2. (*the waned autumnal*) *th'autumnal*
        4. (*winters*) *winter*
        6. *Did my exiled spirit grieve*
        7. (*Sighed . . . sighed*) *Grieved . . . grieved*
      11. (*for*) *and*
      19. (*on*) *o'er*
      20. (*The*) *West*
          (*its*) *thy*
      21. (*O call*) *Oh! call*
          (*highlands*) *lowland*
      22. (*hill-river*) *hill-torrents*
      25. (*darker*) *sullenly*
      32. (*scarlet*) *vermeil*
      33. (*slopes*) *heights*
      34. (*glens*) *crags*
      36. (*that*) *it*
      39. (*dusk*) *dawn*
      42. (*While*) *As*
      52. (*That*) *Which*
      57. (*Its*) *It*
      62. *Than, for me, in that blighted heath lay*
      63. (*that*) *which*
These 1850 alterations are not on the MS.

2   December 4th 1838
    a   2. *The noisy crowd*: *The weary task is put* above l/h
        6. *Full many a land*: *What thought – what scene* above l/h
        7. *And places*: *What spot or* above l/h
        8. *Have* overwritten by *had* p/h
      19. *The garden-walk*: illeg. above [see **c** 1850 line 19 below]
      25. *Yes*: *still* above l/h
      32. *mountains*: illeg. above
      38. *turfy* added l/h
          far and near crossed through: *sweep* at side l/h
      40. *deer* crossed through: *sheep* at side l/h
      44. *I hear my dungeon bars recoil*: *Restraint and heavy task recoil* above l/h
      48. *And given* crossed through; no alternative
          weary care crossed through: *pain and fear* at side l/h
          And brought back labour, task and care underneath l/h
    c   1850 *Stanzas*
        2. *The weary task is put away*
        4. (*A little*) *Alike* (C. misreading)
        6. (*Full many a land*) *What thought, what scene*
        7. (*And places*) *What spot or*
        8. (*Have*) *Has*

14. *Moonless above bends twilight's dome*
19. (*The garden-walk*) *The thorn trees gaunt*
21–4. omitted
25. (*Yet*) *Still*
26. (*flickering*) *alien*
38. (*the path-ways*) *the turfy pathway*
   (*far and near*) *sweep*
40. (*deer*) *sheep*
44. (*I hear my heavy bars recoil*): *Restraint and heavy task recoil*
48. (*And give me back to many a care*): *And back came labour, bondage, care.*

All these 1850 alterations, except to lines 14, 26, are on the MS.

3   December 7th 1838
   a   1. *words*: *words* above 1/h [clarification]
        30. *?yellow* overwritten by *golden* or *golden* crossed through

4   December 18th 1838
   a   5. illeg. overwritten by *spell* p/h
        6. *r* of *drear* crossed out
        25. *?wild/wind*
        39. *?sorrow* crossed through: *longing* at side p/h
        41. *If chilly then the light* crossed through: *Yet oh when chill* (*illeg.*)
            sunbeams above 1/h
        45. *weep* overwritten by *yearn*
   c   1850 ***The Bluebell***
        12. (*The earth its*) *And earth her*
        21. (*heatherbell*) *the sweet bluebell*
        25–40. omitted
        41. (*If chilly then*) *For, oh! when chill*
        42. (*the*) *that*
        43. (*the*) *yon*
        45. (*yearn*) *weep*

Only the 1850 alteration to line 41 is on MS.

5   August 30th 1839
   a   1, 2. The first two lines of poem no. 6 are crossed out and these two
           lines written above them. Emily evidently realized she had
           omitted a poem she wished to include and remedied that
           omission.
        7. *?softly* overwritten by *gently*; ABN *gently* with *softly* above
        11. *from labour's*: illeg. above
        17–24. crossed through by diagonal lines
        25. *proving* of *reproving* crossed through: *Be still* above 1/h
        26. illeg. overwritten by *joys*
        27. *When* partly crossed through: no alternative
            their underlined: *its* above 1/h

6   May 16th 1841
   a   heading *2* (see no. 7 below)
        1. illeg. overwritten by *Earth*

23. *n* of *an* crossed through
The use of 'my' and 'thy' in this poem difficult to distinguish
  c   1850 no title
     23. (*none*) *few*
     24. (*the*) *this*
These 1850 alterations are not on the MS.
   C.'s note: 'The following piece has no title, but in it the Genius of a solitary region seems to address his wandering and wayward votary, and to recall within his influence the proud mind which rebelled at times even against what it most loved.'

7   September 11th 1840
    a   ?***The Night Wind*** [almost illeg.] l/h: cf **c** below
       heading *1* underlined [?linking it with no. 6 above]
       9. illeg. overwritten by *breathing* p/h
      25. ?*W*/*w* in *Wanderer*
      29. illeg. marks above most of the line
      31. *hast loved*: *the solemn* above l/h
      33. *laid at rest* crossed through: *resting* at side p/h
      35. *enough* crossed through
         to altered to *for* p/h
         ing (very faint) added to *mourn* p/h
      36. *to* altered to *for* p/h
         ing added to *be* p/h
    c   1850 ***The Night Wind***
      25. (*leave*) *heed* (C. misreading?)
      29. '*Were we not friends from childhood?*'
      31. *As long as thou the solemn night*
      33. (*laid at rest*) *resting*
      34. (*churchyard*) *church-aisle*
      35. *I* underlined
         (*to mourn*) *for mourning*
      36. *thou* underlined
         (*to be*) *for being*
1850 alterations to lines 29, 31, 33, 35 and 36 are on the MS.
   C.'s note: 'Here again is the same mind [as in poems 6 & 9] in converse with a like abstraction. "The Night Wind", breathing through an open window, has visited an ear which discerned language in its whispers.'

8   March 1st 1841
    a   6. *that* altered to *That*
    c   1846 ***The Old Stoic***
      11. (*Through*) *In*
This 1846 alteration is not on the MS.

9   July 6th 1841
    a 12. ?*As* overwitten by *Like*
    c 1850 no title
      2. *Deep feelings I thought dead*

   3. *Strong in the blast – quick gathering light –*
   4. *The heart's flame kindles red*
   5. (*And*) '*Now*
   6. (*thy kindled*) *thine eyes' full*
   15. (*essence*) *thunder*
   16. *The whisper of its fall*
   17. (*A*) *An*
C. added five lines at the end:
   Nature's deep being, thine shall hold,
   Her spirit all thy spirit fold,
   Her breath absorb thy sighs.
   Mortal! though soon life's tale is told,
      Who once lives, never dies!
and quotation marks beginning at line 5, ending at the last word in the added
stanza.
   Neither the 1850 alterations nor the additional stanza are on the MS.
   C.'s note: 'In these stanzas a louder gale has roused the sleeper on her pillow:
the wakened soul struggles to blend with the storm by which it is swayed.'

10   May 4th 1840
   a   8. *the* overwritten by *a* [1846 *a*]
          14. ?*Shall*/*Should* [1846 *Should*]
   c   1846 *Stanzas*
          11. (*I'm sick to see*) *weary to watch*
This 1846 alteration is not on MS.

12   November 5th 1838
   b   Ash no. 10 has the first three stanzas only, with no title, crossed
          through by diagonal lines.
             3. *thy* (*thine*)
ABN gives no title and dates it 'Nov. 3. 1838'.

13   April 1840
   a   10. ?*cherished* [ABN and Hatfield, but unlike *cherished* as written in the
             next poem, no 14. line 9]
          11. *k* of *know* inked over

14   October 29th 1839
   b   ABN gives no title and dates it 'Oct. 23 1839'.

15   No date
   a   3. *wild* crossed through: *rose* above
   c   1850 ***Love and Friendship***
          No alterations

16   No date
   c   1846 ***Sympathy***
             3. (*sheds*) *pours*
             4. (*Or*) *And*
          11. (*pours its*) *sheds his*

13. (*they*) *these*
15. *man* omitted: *if* added
16. (*But*) *still*

These 1846 alterations are not on the MS.

17   November 14th 1839
    a   9. *?kindly* overwritten by *friendly*
        24. *eye* crossed through: *heart* above
    c   1846 ***Stanzas to* –**
    No alterations.

18   March 1840
    a   23. *g* of *gloom* crossed out, *l* altered to *d* of *doom* p/h
        33. *do* crossed through: *have* above p/h
            dream t added: *dreamt* p/h
            ?rests at crossed through: *lies* above p/h
            a added to *sleep*: *asleep* p/h

19   July 17th 1841
    a   1. smudged *?pitteous*; ABN *piteous*
        30. *?endless*: *mindless* Hatfield: ABN's suggestion, *boundless*, seems unlikely

20   October 23rd – 42 – February 6th 1843 [sic]
    a   3. *v* of *have* overwritten by *s* (*has*)
        15. *Yet* crossed through: *weak* added above between *still* and *repentance* p/h
        22. *says* crossed through: *sobs* above p/h
        24. *Says would'st thou longer* crossed through: *Canst thou desire to* underneath p/h
        31. crossed through illeg.: *brave* above p/h
        38. crossed through, illeg.: *Has dared what few would dare* above p/h
        39. *dare* crossed through: *done* above p/h
        40. *Yet* overwritten by *But*
        46/7. two words interlined illeg.
    c   1846 ***Self-interrogation***
        13. (*I think*) *I've said*
        15. (*weak*) *sad*
        40. (*Yet*) *But*
        43. (*'Twill be*) *It is*
        44. (*be*) *seem*
        45. (*fight*) *war*
        47. (*Thine eventide*) *Thy midnight rest*
        48. *And break in glorious morn.*

These 1846 alterations are not on the MS.

21   December 18th 184–
    a ***Hope*** (added by whom? – unusual p/h)
        2. *my* crossed through: *the* above p/h
        12. *When* crossed through: *If* above p/h

    c   1846 ***Hope***
         18. (*that*) *my*
This 1846 alteration is not on MS.

22   February 10th 1844
    a   ***My Comforter***
         6. *breast/heart* scribbled out: *soul* at side p/h
         9. *light* overwritten by *ray*
        17. *With*: ?*Their* above
        18. *Their* overwritten by *Whose*: *maddening* altered to *maddened* p/h
        19. *And* crossed out: no alternative
        24. *gr* of *groan* altered to *m*(*moan*)
        27. *zephyr o'er* crossed through: *air above* above p/h
        28. illeg. overwritten by *tossed* p/h
           illeg. print under the last line of the poem
    c   1846 ***My Comforter***
        12. (*unlit*) *alone*
        17. (*With*) *their*
        18. *Whose madness daily maddened me*
        19. (*And turning*) *Distorting*
        25. (*Thy. . .thy*) *My. . .my*
        31. (*can match with*) *resembles*
Only the 1846 alterations to lines, 17, 18 are on the MS.

23   April 13th 1843.
    a   22. (*th*)*at* altered to (*th*)*e*
        30. *was* overwritten by *is*
        36. *sh* written above *sh*(*ortest*) l/h [?clarification]
        40. *while* [?E.'s copying error] *whole*
    c   1846 ***How Clear She Shines***
        2. (*silver*) *guardian*
        10. (*go hide*) *conceal*
        30. (*is*) *was*
        31. (*his*) *her*
        36. (*shortest*) *surest*
These 1846 alterations are not on the MS.

24   March 5th 1844
    a   26. ?*lights* crossed through: *things* above p/h
        44. *every where* crossed through: *far and near* at side p/h
        67. ?*would not*: *would'st* [1846]
    c   1846 ***A Day Dream***
        16. (*Asked, 'what do you do here?'*) *Asked, 'What do you here?'*
        35. (*the Fall*) *its Fall*
        36. (*its*) *the*
        41. (*glancing*) *gleaming*
        49. (*rang*) *rung*
        67. *would not* [1846 *wouldst* – which reverses the meaning]

68. *Because* printed in italics
These 1846 alterations are not on the MS.

25   September 3rd 1844
    a heading ***To Imagination*** p/h (of a kind)
        12. *Hath* overwritten by *Have*
        21. *tells s* crossed off
        30. *?other* crossed through: *real* above p/h
        33. *dying* crossed through: *failing* at side p/h
    c 1846 ***To Imagination***
        14. (*grief*) *guilt*
        16. (*unsullied*) *untroubled*
        26. (*visions*) *vision*
        36. (*brighter*) *sweeter*
These 1846 alterations are not on the MS.

26   October 14th 1844
    a 10. *?thus* overwritten by *did*
        16. *?things* altered to *Beings*
        21. *willing* crossed through: *ready* above p/h
        34. *my* crossed through: *a* above p/h
    c 1846 ***Plead for Me***
        20. *mine* in italics
        33. (*real*) *earthly*
These 1846 alterations are not on the MS.

27   February 3d [sic] 1845
    a 3. *thy* altered to *this*
        7–14. underlined on the MS
        15. *say* altered to *said*; illeg. overwritten by *I*
        26. illeg. overwritten by *suffer*
        32. *and* squeezed in at the beginning of the line
        37. *lighting* crossed through: *kyndling* [sic] above p/h
        38. illeg. crossed through: *deep* above p/h
            far and crossed through: *wide and bright* at side p/h
        39. illeg. altered to *far*
        40. *their* overwritten by *its*
        46. *Once* underlined in MS
        51. illeg. crossed through: *Implored* above p/h
            illeg. overwritten by *change*
            illeg. overwritten by *lifeless*
        53. *But* crossed through: *O* above
        53–6. original lines scored out: replaced by present lines 53–6 which are squeezed in before the next poem over-running the lines E. always draws at the end of each poem.
        For the cancelled lines Hatfield makes the following suggestion which, as far as one can see, may well be correct.
        O for the lid that cannot weep
        The breast that needs no breath –

The tomb that brings eternal sleep –
To Life's Deliverer, Death!

Hatfield notes that the title, *The Philosopher's Conclusion*, has been added in pencil at the head of the poem. There is no sign of this on the SHB facsimile.

c   1846 ***The Philosopher***
35.   (*bent*) *sent*
36.   (*on*) *through*
46.   *once* in italics
51.   (*lifeless*) *senseless*
55.   (*vanquished*) *conquered*: (*victorious*) *conquering*

These 1846 alterations are not on the MS.

28   April 14th 1845
a   2.   *my = thy*
c   1846 ***Stars***
2.   (*my/thy*) *our*
17.   (*rise*) *dawn*
24.   *mine* in italics
27.   (*bathe*) *steep.*

These 1846 alterations are not on the MS.

29   April 10th 1845
a   25.   *Heartless* crossed through before *death*: illeg. above [1846 *cruel*]
31.   *may* overwritten by *will*
c   1846 ***Death***
20.   (*its*) *that*

This 1846 alteration is not on the MS.

30   June 2d [sic] 1845
a   21.   illeg. overwritten by *trustfull* [sic] p/h
35.   illeg. overwritten by *Nor* p/h
36.   ?*With: In* above crossed through p/h [1846 *With*]
41.   *for* crossed through: *in* above p/h

Bottom of MS is faintly written: 'Never was better. . .(illeg.) . . . nd' p/h.
Hatfield notes this as a comment by Charlotte giving it as: 'Never was better stuff penned'

c   1846 ***Anticipation***
4.   (*shadowy*) *unreal*
12.   (*fortunes*) *fortune*
14.   (*dull, unlovely*) *clouded, smileless*
15.   (*had they*) *if they*
(*unproved*) *untried*
16.   (*were wildly wrung*) *went wandering wrong*
26.   (*will*) *must*
48.   *Sustained, my guide, by thee*
50.   (*springs*) *swells*

These 1846 alterations are not on the MS.

31   Jan 2nd 1846

    a   2. ?*from* crossed through (between *in* and *the*): no alternative
               illeg. overwritten by *troubled*

        8. ?*strength* overwritten by *power*

     12. illeg. overwritten by *amid*

     22. *shine* crossed through: *be* at side p/h

     24. illeg. overwritten by *Existence*
           thine crossed through: *thee* at side

     28. *will* overwritten by *may*

    c   1850 ***No Coward Soul Is Mine***

      7. (*hast*) *has*

    14. (*thy*) *thine*

    21. (*moon*) *man*

    23. (*thou*) *Thou*

    27. (*Since thou*) *Thou* – *THOU*

    28. (*thou*) *THOU*

These 1846 alterations are not on the MS.

   C.'s note: 'The following are the last lines my sister Emily ever wrote.' (This is incorrect – see Gon nos. 43, 44 dated '14 September 1846', 'May 13th 1847/?8' [Hatfield 1848] – though each of these poems is in an unfinished state.

Chronological order of poems

12, 1, 2, 3, 4, 5, 14, 15, 16, 17, 18, 13, 10, 11, 7, 8, 6, 9, 19, 20, 23, 21, 22, 24, 25, 26, 27, 29, 28, 30, 31.

Gondal MS

One of the two Notebooks of 1844 is dedicated to Gondal, Emily and Anne's imaginary other world. The title to this MS is adorned with a pattern of trailing leaves and flourishes. There are several approaches that can engage the reader's interest in these poems. There are the bedevilling attempts to set the poems comfortably into a total Gondal saga: there is the aligning of the poems with the novel, *Wuthering Heights*, revealing how the tones and attitudes of the one reflect the other: and there is the assessment of the poems, critically, as lyrics in themselves. With the increasing critical exploration of the Brontës, and particularly of their juvenilia, the reading of these poems as quasi autobiography has happily ended.

Although there is some help in the grouping by Emily of the poems (nos. 1–9, 16–18 are concerned with A.G.A. and her relationships, to be followed later by the ballad of her death, 21, and a lament, 23; nos., 11–14 concentrate on Julius Brenzaida, (for whom, and not for Branwell, as was once thought, the fine lament, no. 36, was composed), no format seems to encompass all the poems snugly. This approach, even though it may be fun, engaging one's wits and curiosity, can prove time-consuming and its ultimate value is questionable.

The second approach has perhaps more relevance. Certainly, in the poems dealing with Samara, can be found tones and attitudes similar to those of Heathcliff, as, in the A.G.A. and Rosina poems, there are elements of Cathy. More than this, the antitheses between light and dark, fair and blackhaired, conventional and outcast, with their reversal in subsequent generations, are prominent in both poems and novel. And, in both, over and around all, plays or broods the moorland terrain. Certainly any lingering doubts as to the authorship of *Wuthering Heights* must founder on the telling presence of these common qualities.

However it is as lyrics in themselves that these poems must stand or fall. They share with Byron, Shelley and Sir Walter Scott, amongst others, a commitment to the narrative lyric, where the poem is either its own story or, as song or lyric, is a comment on or is contained by the story in which it appears. Though there is little doubt that the 'peculiar music' of her poetry is more obviously present in the poems of the EJB Notebook, many of the poems (nos. 9, 21, 36 and 42 for example) have that unique voice with which Emily Brontë's poetry speaks to her readers.

Emily has added her initials at the side of the headings to many of the poems (nos. 2–8, 10–23, 25–27, 31, 33–34) in this MS. These are not recorded.

1   *A.G.A.*, March 6th 1837
    a   17. *that* overwritten by *who*
         23. illeg. overwritten by *gold*
         62. illeg. overwritten by *smiled*
         64. *joy* crossed through: *bloom* at side p/h
         66. *Above* illeg. *my* illeg. *tomb*: *unremembered* above p/h
         67–8. two lines crossed through (illeg.): present lines 67–8 underneath
         p/h
         ***[sic at end]

2   *A.G.A. to A.E.* August 19th 1837
    a   9. ?*lovely* = *lonely*
    b   Bonn 6 ***Song***
         3. *dawning (the dawn)*
         8. *Moans (Waves)*
         9. *noble (?lonely)*
        11. *Shining (Gleaming)*
        15. *step (foot)*
        17. *the (a)*
        18. *Thinking of (Parted from)*: *grieving for (parted from)*
        19. *Longing to be in sweet Elbë again*
        20. *Thinking and grieving and longing in vain*
         This version is cancelled by diagonal lines.
        Ash 1 contains the last five lines only: with 'Emily Jane Brontë –
        August 19th 1837' at the end
        18, 19, 20. as in Bonn: interlined
        Parted from Gondal and parted from me above p/h
        All my repining is hopeless and vain underneath p/h
        Death never gives back his victims again underneath p/h

3   *A.G.A. to A.S.* May 6th 1840, July 28th 1843
    a   13. illeg. overwritten by *Reflects*
         20. ?*dreary* crossed through: *coldly* above p/h
         28. *would* crossed through: *can* above p/h
         37. *nd* of *And* crossed through: *A*

4   *To A.G.A.* undated
    b   Bonn 3 and 8
        Bonn 3
         1. *I'm standing in the forest now*
         3. *green (fresh)*; *gleam* crossed through: alternative underneath illeg.
         4. *that (the)*
         8. crossings out, illeg: *towerlike   tentlike* above
         9. final version of an additional stanza, subsequently rejected:

           The murmur of their boughs and streams
            Speaks pride as well as bliss,
            And that blue heaven expanding seems
            The circling hills to kiss.

11. *No – whisper not to me –*
12. *dreamer* (*Lady*)
16. *?is* blotted out
18. *and you deride* (*whate'er betide*)
19. *changeless* (*faithful*)
21. *ocean's* (*rolling*)
22. *trouble* (*sorrow*)
26–7. *I dreamt one dark and stormy night*
    When winter winds were wild
Bonn 8 contains lines 26–33 only
28. *?radiant* (*ardent*)
29. *And* (*Then*)

5   ***A.G.A. to A.S.*** March 2d [sic] 1844
   a   6. *be gone* crossed through: *depart* above p/h
         11. *might* crossed through: *may* above p/h
         12. *?will* crossed through: *may* above p/h
         13. illeg. altered to *will* p/h
         15. *Yet* overwritten by *But* p/h
            illeg. overwritten by *no grief can I* p/h
         17. *But* overwritten by *Yet* p/h
         19. *When* crossed through: *And* above p/h
         21–4. original four lines crossed through, illeg.: present lines 21–4
            interlined p/h

6   ***A.G.A. to A.S.*** May 20th 1838
   a   9. illeg. crossed through: *small* above p/h
   b   Ash 5 ***Lines by A.G.A. to A.S.***
      6. *Sweet* (*Young*): *are* (*look*)
      9. *Our* (*The*)
      10. *throstle* (*stockdove*)
      18. *shall* (*must*)
ABN misreads E. May 20 1838 as February 20 1838

7   ***A.G.A. To the Bluebell*** May 9th 1839
   b   Ash 7 ***To a Bluebell by A.G.A.***
      7. *fair* crossed through: *wan* above p/h
      9. *Lift thy head and speak to me*
      10. *thoughts* (*words*)
      11. *whisper* (*murmur*)
      12. *Lights my course commenced and done* or
         Lights me till my life is done above p/h
      14. *cruel* crossed through: *stormy* (*ruthless*)
      16. *Dews of heaven are round me shed*
This version is crossed through by diagonal lines.

8   ***Written in Aspin Castle*** August 20th 1842, February 6th 1843
   a   8. ABN *Beckden's*, Hatfield *Rockden's*

14. illeg. *the* above p/h
21. *glen* crossed through: *cliff* at side p/h
   gnarled tree in margin l/h (clarification)
26–8. three lines crossed through, illeg.: replaced by present lines 26–8
30. *this* = *the*
50. *Beneath* crossed through: *Under* above p/h
82. *in exile* crossed through: *unsheltered* above p/h

9   ***Douglases*** [sic] ***Ride*** July 11th 1838
   a   2. *organ's* crossed through: ?*music's* above l/h
      12. illeg. overwritten by *pressed*
      33. *Roared*: *roared* above l/h [clarification]
      34. ABN *From*, Hatfield *drops* (*Brought*)
      50. ABN/Hatfield *dare*
      61. ABN *rising* (*nearing*)
      64. illeg. overwritten by *laid by* p/h
         men: *men* above l/h [clarification]
      69. ?*as* crossed through: *when* above

10   ***By R. Gleneden*** April 17th 1839
   a   13. *grieving* crossed through: *weeping* at side p/h
      41. *eve*: *eve* above l/h [clarification]
   b   Ash 13 Contains lines 1–3, 34–44: the rest is missing
      35. *Tay and Carlo* (*Listlessly they*)
      38. *woe* (*pain*)
      42. illeg. crossed through: *hall* above.
These lines are lightly crossed through by diagonal lines. ABN title ***The Absent One*** and date April 19th 1839:

11   –

12   ***Rosina*** 2' [sic] September 1st 1841
   a   2', Is this a second poem dealing with Rosina or a second Rosina or merely an addendum by another hand?

13   ***Song by Julius Brenzaida to G.S.*** October 17th 1838
      ABN title **Song** and date October 19th 1838

14   ***Song by Julius Brenzaida to G.S.*** October 17th 1838.
   a   *Love's Farewell* added underneath title
      5. *moor* crossed through: *hill* above l/h
      7. ?*my* overwritten by *your*
      10. *rosey*: *falsest* above l/h
      11. *prison*: ?*strongest* above l/h
   c   1850 **Last Words**
      4. (*My slighted*) *My lips or*
      5. (*moorside*) *hillside*
      10. (*rosey*) *falsest*
      14. (*prison*) *strongest*

The 1850 alterations to lines 5, 10, 14 are on the MS.

15   *Geraldine* [flourish] August 17th 1841
    a   42. Hatfield *change (charge)*
The last stanza is squashed in with the last line overlapping into the title of 16.

16   *A.G.A.*, August 30th 1838
    a   *The Lady to her Guitar* added underneath the title l/h
        2. *Has = Hast = Hath* overwritten
        5. *t* of *It* underlined
        8. *wrapt* overwritten by *wrapped*
        12. *gleaming* crossed through: *Dryad* underneath l/h
        14. *Has = Hast = Hath* overwritten: *wakened*: *wakened* above   l/h
        [clarification]
        15. *Has = Hast = Hath* overwritten
    c   1850 **The Lady to Her Guitar**
        2. *(hast) has* [see above]
        7. *(tempest and) storm or shades*
        8. *(Had) Have*
        12. *(gleaming) Dryad*
        14. *Hath* [see above]
        15. *Hath* [see above]
Only the title and li 12 are altered on the MS.

17   *F. De Samara. Written in the Gaaldine prison caves. To A.G.A.*
January 6th 1840
    a   32. *hide* overwritten by *blot*
        53. illeg. overwritten by *Lethian*

18   –

19   *Written on returning to the P. of I. on the 10th of January* 1827
June 14th 1839
    a   7. *?doth* altered to *does*
        16. *Their* in italics – E.'s p/h version
    b   Howe 14 contains the first six lines only: cancelled by lines across
        1. *glided (hurried)*
        2–6 as in present text

20   *On the Fall of Zalona* February 24th 1843
    a   31. '*Zalona*. . there are no closing quotation marks in the MS: ?after
        die
        45. *unbroken thus*: *unbroken thus* above l/h [clarification]

21   *A.G.A. The Death of* January 1841–May 1844
    a   7. *their* crossed through: *each* above p/h
        s of *belts* crossed through: *belt*
        illeg. crossed out: *a* above p/h
        s of *weapons* crossed through: *weapon*
        8. *were* overwritten by *was*
        60. *All* underlined: *rue* at side l/h [clarification]

74. *illeg.* partly crossed through: *?I* remains: poss. originally *me* but in correcting the grammar, E. loses the rhyme
75. *glittering* crossed through: *?radiant* [ABN and Hatfield] above p/h *glittering* retained in text as it, at least, is legible
77. *illeg.* overwritten by *dwelt* p/h
143. *Surry* [sic]
204. *?south* overwritten by *soft* p/h
237. *quietly* underlined: *all quiet* in margin l/h
271. *uncovered* in margin l/h [clarification]
286. *treason*: *treason* l/h at side [clarification]
337. *passed = past*
341. *vain*: *vain* in margin l/h [clarification]

22   *A Farewell to Alexandria* July 12th 1839(?8)
   a   18. *?my* [ABN]
         28. *my* crossed through, no alternative
Emily's writing of '*my*' and '*thy*' is particularly difficult to differentiate in this poem. For alternative readings, see Hatfield.

23   *E.W. to A.G.A.* March 11th 1844
   a   *On a life perverted* added underneath the title p/h [? E.'s]
         14. *illeg.* overwritten by *where*
         15. *illeg.* overwritten by *memory* [see below **c** 1850 line 15]
         31. *urged* crossed through: *bore* above p/h
         35. *grieved* crossed through: *wept* above
         37. *illeg.* overwritten by *recks* p/h
   c   1850 ***The Wanderer from the Fold***
         14. *(Love and gladness) sinless sunshine*
         15. *(Memory) presence*
         16. *Like gladsome summer-day*
         20. *(That) Which*
         31. *(That) Which*
These 1850 alterations are not on the MS.

24   –

25   *Date 18 – E.G. to M.R.* May 4th 1843
   a   *A Serenade* added underneath the heading p/h
         11. *honour*: *true love* above l/h
         12. *illeg.* crossed through: *fears* above p/h
         23. *Gleneden's*: *for honour's* above: *for honour's* in margin l/h [clarification]

26   *To A.S.* 1830 May 1st 1843
   a   2. ABN *hours*, Hatfield *noons*
       ABN title ***Grave in the Ocean***

27   Title *illeg.* and crossed through, E. September 6th 1843
   a   *Warning and Reply* added underneath the title l/h
         11. *?all* blotted out no alternative: 1850 *all*

13. underlined in MS
15. underlined in MS
23. *?broke* altered to *breaks*
    there crossed through: *here* at side 1/h
24. *But* added at begining of line 1/h; *That* underlined in MS
c 1850 ***Warning and Reply***
8. (*twined*) *entwined*
12. (*its gloom and thee*) *shudderingly*
15. (*they'll*) *they will*
23. (*broke*) *breaks*: (*there*) *here*
24. *But* added at beginning of the line

The 1850 alterations to lines 23, 24 are on the MS.

28   ***A.S. to G.S.*** . . . . December 19th 1841
a   *Encouragement* added underneath the title 1/h [cf **c** 1850]
14. *Gerald* crossed through: *sister* above 1/h
c   1850 *Encouragement*
14. (*Gerald*) *sister*
21. (*well*) *thou*

The 1850 alteration to line 14 is on the MS.

29   ***M.G. for the U.S.*** December 19th 1843
a   16. illeg. overwritten by *scattered*
24. *hours*: *hours* above 1/h [clarification]

30   *?9?G* May 1st 1844
a   19. *s* of *Dwellers* crossed through: *Dweller*
20. *Are* crossed through: *Is* above p/h
E.W. [sic] at end of the poem
c   1846 *Song*

No alterations.

31   ***From a Dungeon Wall in the Southern College – JB. Sept 1825 –***
Nov 11th 1844
a   *T* [sic] *Old Man's Lecture* added underneath the title 1/h/
c   1850 ***The Elder's Rebuke***
An extract of lines 1–28 only
5 and 6. linked making one stanza of lines 1–12
8. (*these*) *those*
10. (*ears*) *ear*
14. (*serious power*) 'serious power' [sic]
28. Hatfield *tears*, C. *fears* (tears)

C. adds six lines:
Thus spake the ice-blooded elder gray;
The young man scoffed as he turned away,
Turned to the call of the sweet lute's measure,
Waked by the lightsome touch of plesure:
Had he ne'er met a gentle teacher,
Woe had been brought by that pitiless preacher.

These 1850 alterations are not on the MS.

ABN title **Love's Rebuke**; includes lines 35 to the end of poem only. He, evidently transcribed the remainder of the poem after C. had taken what she wanted for her 1850 volume. She herself had omitted lines 29–34, which would have proved muddling when lines 1–28 were published separately.

32   *From a D.W. in the N.C. A.G.A. Sept. 1826* Dec 2d [sic] 1844
    a   D–W– = Dungeon Wall; N.C. = North College
        3. *tranquil* crossed through: *glorious* above p/h
        4. *gloriously* crossed through: *tranquilly* above p/h
      11. illeg. overwritten by *warm*
           illeg. overwritten by *Arden* (both as 1846)
      13. *Beside thee on* crossed through: alternative crossed out illeg.
           bended crossed through: no alternative; 1846 Beside thee on my knee
      14. *own* crossed through: *dearest* squashed in
      22. illeg. crossed out: *Eden isles* above p/h
      24. illeg. crossed out: *?own* above p/h (as 1846)
      27. *?No* overwritten by *?Nay* [as 1846]
           ?Elbë [cf. Gon 1] overwritten by *?Edward* [as 1846]
    37–44. a passage so overwritten and crossed through it is impossible to log all the alterations clearly in the Notes. Most of it can only be understood by reference to the 1846 volume, for which it seems probable it was altered. The legible lines remaining are as given in the text. Except for a few minor variations and ignoring the punctuation and lack of capital letters at the beginning of the lines, the legible words are those of the 1846 volume.
    c   1846 ***A Death Scene***
        9. (*Elbë*) *Edward*
      16. *one* no underlining
      27. (*?Elbë*) *Edward*
      39. (*gentle*) *twilight*
      43. (*light*) *orbs*
Only the alteration to line 27 is, smudged and almost illegible, on the MS.

33   *D.G.C. to J.A.* October 2d [sic] 1844.
    a 17. *?bear*

34   *I.M. to I.G.* November 6th 1844
    a   8. *?fain*, 1846 *faint*: ?E miscopy
    c   1846 ***Faith and Despondency***
        4. (*closing*) *gathering*
        7. (*blasts*) *gusts*
      19. (*gather*) *closes*
      22. (*speechless*) *hopeless*
      24. (*see*) *greet*
      51. (*roots*) *root*
      54. (*lies asleep*) *rest in sleep*
      65. (*coming*) *worldly*
These 1846 alterations are not on the MS.

35   ***M. Douglas to E. R. Gleneden*** November 21st 1844.
    c   1846 ***Honour's Martyr***
        21. (*Beside*) *Without*
        33. (*venomed*) *covert*
        47. (*that*) *that* [in italics]
        52. (*name*) *name* [in italics]
        56. (*Gleneden*) *Then, only then*
These 1846 alterations are not on the MS.

36   ***R Alcona to J Brenzaida*** March 3d. [sic] 1845
    a   8. *thy* crossed through: *that* above p/h
        20. *the*; 1846 *thee*
        31. ?*delightful* crossed through: *divinest* above p/h
    c   1846 ***Remembrance***
        4. (*all wearing*) *all-severing*
        6. (*Angora's*) *that northern*
        8. (*That*) *Thy*
        15. (*Sterner*) *Other*: (*darker*) *other*
        17. (*No other sun*) *No later light*
        18. (*No other star*) *No second morn*
These 1846 alterations are not on the MS.

37   ***H.A. and A.S.*** May 17th 1842
    a   6–8. *who now has raven hair*
             And those eyes rival dark of night
             were once as morning fair in margin l/h
        7. ?*scowls*; Hatfield *locks*
        11. illeg. *grief* overwritten by *agony* p/h
        19. ?*death* crossed through before *pale*
        22. *beats*: *once beat* above l/h
        23. *soft ringlets lightly rest* crossed through: *heart found a living rest* underneath l/h
        24. *And move* crossed through: *That ?turned?moved?heard* underneath l/h
        27. *Gondal's* crossed through: *England's* above l/h
        28. *arched* at side l/h [clarification]
           Gondal's crossed through: *English* underneath l/h
        32. *That* overwritten by *Which*
        36. in the margin between stanzas l/h:
           Whose then illeg. [Hatfield *the arms*]
           whose the eyes
           That clasp and watch her now
        48. *storm-cleared* in margin l/h [clarification]

38   ***Rodric Lesley 1830*** Dec 18th 1843.
    a   *Roderic* added underneath the title l/h
        10. *hundreds*: *many* above l/h
        20. *thy monarch's legions* crossed through: *thy war worn comrades* above l/h
        ABN title ***Roderic***.

39   No title, April 22d [sic] 1845.

   a   4. *quenched* crossed through: *hushed* above p/h

          24. illeg. crossed through: *spirits* above p/h

          25. illeg. crossed through: *all* above p/h

          29. *The ardent and the happy breast* squeezed in after line 28 p/h

          30. *life = hope* p/h

          36. illeg. overwritten by *last* p/h

40   ***A.E. and R.C.*** May 28th 1845.

   a   *The Two Children* added above the title l/h

         6. *And* crossed through: no alternative

       18. illeg. overwritten by *sombre*

       33. *?Brothers* crossed through; above illeg. crossed through; *orphan* above l/h [Is this by E. or a clarification; *orphan*, see text, makes more sense, but this is not necessarily a sound criterion]

       37. *golden* crossed through: *sunbright* above p/h

       41. illeg. crossed through: *spring* at side p/h

       51. *And* crossed through: no alternative

       52. *?beamy* smudged

       59. *my* (between *but* and *love*) crossed through: no alternative

      NB. This is all one poem in the MS.

   c   1850 ***The Two Children***

      Printed as two separate poems, lines 1–36 and 37–60

       7. (*beats*) *throbs*

      19. *Boyhood sad is merging*

      20. (*sterner*) *In sadder*

      23. (*unknowing*) *unconcious*

      25. (*Blossoms*) *Blossom*

      27. (*your*) *thy*

      28. (*Your*) *Thy*

      31. (*your*) *thy*

      32. (*the*) *a*

      33. (*orphan, wither*) *soul and blossom*

      34. (*You were*) *You both were*

      43. (*thy*) *thine*

      44. (*Borne*) *wafted*

      46. (*And I do not*) *Nor do I*

      51. *And I vowed – if need were – to share his sadness*

      52. (*beamy*) *sunny*

      56. after this line C. added:

            '*Watch in love by a feverish pillow,*

            Cooling the fever with pity's balm;

            Safe as the petrel on tossing billow,

            Safe in mine own soul's golden calm!

      60. (*And more unsleeping*) *And my* (in italics) *love is truer*

Neither the 1850 alterations nor the additions are on the MS.

41   ***M.A. Written on the Dungeon Wall. N C*** August 1845

   a   12. illeg. overwritten by *cloud*

M.A. written at the end of the poem.

42   *Julian M. and A. G. Rochelle* October 9th 1845
  a   *The Signal Light* added underneath the title l/h
        26. illeg. overwritten by *sculptured*
        30. there are no quotation marks after *struck'* or before *'and I. . .*
        42. there are no quotation marks after *friend'* or before *'you. . .*
        51. *too* (before *wildy*) crossed through
        54. illeg. overwritten by *playmates*
        64–5. *Still let my tyrants know* added between p/h
        83. illeg. *Its wings are almost free* above p/h
        85–9. no inverted commas
        147. *Yet = But*
        151. illeg. crossed through: *unswerving* above p/h
  c   1846 ***The Prisoner, a Fragment***
        This is an extract of lines 13–44 (marked by a *, a line down the
        lefthand margin and *Pubd*) and lines 65–92 (marked by lines)
        40. *(which) that*
        43. *(parent's) kindred's*
        65. *(Yet, tell them, Julian, all) Still, let my tyrants know* [see above]
        72. *(which) that*
        85. *(O) Oh*
        93. Four lines added to complete the poem as published, the first line
            of which is a variation of line 93 in the MS:
            (I) We (watched her there) turned to go
            We had no further power to work the captive woe;
            Her cheek, her gleaming eye, declared that man had given
            A sentence unapproved and overruled by Heaven.
Neither the 1846 alterations to lines 43, 72, 85, 93 nor the additions are on the
MS.
        1850 ***The Visionary***
        This is an extract of lines 1–12 only
          4. *(drifts) drift*
        12. *(winter) frozen*
After this line C. has added:

> *What I love shall come like visitant of air,*
> *Safe in secret power from lurking human snare;*
> *What love's me, no word of mine shall e'er betray*
> *Though faith for faith unstained my life must forfeit pay.*
>
> *Burn, then, little lamp; glimmer straight and clear –*
> *Hush! a rustling wing stirs, methinks, the air:*
> *He for whom I wait, thus ever comes to me;*
> *Strange Power! I trust thy might; trust thou my constancy.*

Neither the 1850 alterations nor the additions are on the MS.

43   No title, 14 September 1846
        Both 43 and 44 are part copied up and part newly written. In 43, from line
        149 the text grows increasingly difficult to read. There is little or no

punctuation. What I have offered in the text is my own reading of what is reasonably legible. For the rest, where I agree that Hatfield's conjectures are possible, I have entered them in the text in brackets; otherwise I have left blanks and listed Hatfield's suggestions in the Notes.

Even merely to list all the alterations would make the notes as unintelligible as the MS itself often is. Up to line 148, therefore, I offer only the variants that are legible; after line 148 I offer only my reading of the MS with no attempt at punctuation – there is none in the MS. For the problems these two poems occasion, I refer you to the illustration elsewhere in this book. All the alterations are in p/h.

a   (to line 148)

1. *seek* crossed through: *ask* above
3. crossed through illeg.: *crushed the helpless even as we* part above, part below the line
7. crossed through illeg.: *look on* above
8. *As* crossed through: *with* above
   illeg. crossed through: *sympathy* above
11. *by* crossed through: *after* above
13. *one* crossed through: *a* above
18. *reeking* crossed through: *human* above
27. *And more . . . tell thee* crossed through: *And. . . confess that* above
36. crossed through illeg.: *seek* at side
52. illeg. overwritten by *distress*
54. *Anguish* crossed through: *A doom*
60. crossed through illeg.: *nerved* at side
61. crossed through illeg. [between *To* and *deeds*]: no alternative
   crossed through illeg.: *from which the desperate swerved* part above, part at side of the line
62. crossed through illeg.: *tell* above
71. *dusker* (*duskier*)
83. crossed through illeg. above: *weak* underneath
85. *How* crossed through: *For* above
86. illeg. overwritten by *But*
   heard crossed through: *saw* above
87. *Fiend-like* crossed through: *harshly* above, *coldly* below
88. crossed through illeg.: *Now* above
91. *gh* of *though* crossed through: *thou*
101. *?sleep* crossed through: *live* above
109. *?strike* crossed through: two other illeg. words crossed through: *smite* below: *proud* crossed through: no alternative
124. *him* crossed through: *his* at side; illeg. crossed through: *?ghostly? ghastly* above
131. *Night following night* or *Through the long* alternative below
134. *?the laughing* crossed through: *returning* above
138. *?urgent* [Hatfield *west*]
144. crossed through illeg.: *?lightness* above
148. crossed through illeg.: *doubtful* above

Hatfield's suggestions (where in the text I have left spaces):

169. *my enemy*
191. *one breath*
193. *wildered*
206. *helpless*
235. *He*
250. *soul*
252–3. omitted
261/2. omitted
265. *full*
266. *me. . . .we*

44 No title, May 13th 1848
   a   1. illeg: *Why ask to know* above
       3. illeg. crossed through: illeg. above crossed through: *power* at side
       4. illeg. crossed through: *foot-kissers* underneath; *prosperous* crossed through: *triumphant* above
       5. crossed through illeg.; *crushers* at side; crossed through illeg.: *helpless* above
       8. two, (possibly three) lines crossed through illeg. [see lines 8, 9 of present text]
     10. illeg. crossed through: *senseless* above
     15. *which* crossed through: *That* at side: altered to *The*
     16. alternative *But we with heedless unregarding eyes*
     17. original line crossed through illeg. [?replaced by present line 17]
     21. *And ground beyond* crossed through [?rejected start to line 21]
     21–5. a stain obliterates much of these lines
     Hatfield's suggestions:
     9. *cursers*
    18. omitted
    21. *and*
    22. *ears*
    23. *of hoofs*
    24. *on*

These two poems are the last, extant, poems E. wrote. Doubtless their incomplete state – they are not transcribed final versions but working texts – as well as the romantic clarion call of the poem she allotted to that place, lead C. to disregard them when she claimed 'No Coward Soul Is Mine' (Jan 2nd 1846 EJB 31) to be the last poem her sister ever wrote.

Chronological order of poems

1, 2, 6, 11, 9, 16, 13, 14, 18, 10, 7, 19, 24, 4, 17, 3, 21, 15, 12, 28, 37, 8, 20, 26, 25, 27, 38, 29, 5, 23, 24, 30, 33, 34, 31, 35, 32, 36, 39, 40, 41, 42, 43, 44.

Appendix 1

Glossary

There are references to dates, places and characters of the Gondal saga in the poems, the 'Diaries' and Anne's lists of places (in a copy of Goldsmith's *Geography*). Most of what can be learnt about Gondal is a matter of deduction as there are no prose manuscripts extant to provide the necessary background. This is not the place for a detailed presentation of the arguments and conclusions reached.* However, the contrast between the North Island (Gondal), with its harsh winter climate, its flora and fauna, all akin to those of Yorkshire, and the more southerly Gaaldine, with its seductive blue skies, hot suns and palm trees, as well as the contrasts between the characters who inhabit them – raven-haired, dark-eyed, passionate opposed to fair-haired, blue-eyed, gentle but dull – is as much a part of the poems as it is of the later novel, *Wuthering Heights*.

The Dating of the Saga

From the few dates that can be culled from the poems, it seems the saga was set in the early 1800s. 'The History of the Glasstown Confederacy' of Branwell and Charlotte starts in 1770 when the Twelves (Branwell's toy soldiers) set out to explore and colonize a part of Africa. What relationship, in its beginnings, Gondal bore to Glasstown, or when exactly its invention came about (it must have been well established by 1834 when the Gondalians are mentioned in Emily and Anne's 'Diary') we do not know though, as in a considerable amount of Brontë criticism, deductions/guesses have been made.

The Glossary

This glossary covers references to characters and places mentioned in this book. Wherever relevant, information from other sources (i.e. other poems, the 'Diaries', the lists) is also used. The numbers refer to the number of the poem in the Gondal Notebook. Those with 'A' in front refer to those in the Ashley Notebook. Where there are only initials given, the last letter is deemed to be the first letter of the surname and is placed accordingly (e.g. D.G.C. is C., D.G.).

Dates given in the poems:

18—	no. 25
1825	no. 31
1826	no. 32
1827	no. 19
1830	no. 26
1830	no. 38
the passage of 15 years	no. 36

*see for this, Fannie Ratchford, *The Gondal Story* and *Emily's Poems Arranged as an Epic of Gondal*, both in the Introduction to C. W. Hatfield (ed.), *The Complete Poems of Emily Brontë*, Columbia University Press, 1941, and *Gondal's Queen*, Texas, 1955; W. D. Paden, *An Investigation of Gondal*, New York, 1958. For information about the Glasstown Confederacy see *The Early Writings of Charlotte Brontë* Christine Alexander, Basil Blackwell, 1983.

A., A. a dark-haired child taken across the sea by his/her mother [A6]

A., A.A. a boy doomed to be hell-like in misery [A12]

A., A.G. (**Augusta Geraldine Alme(i)da**) an important character; brought up with **Angelica**; in love with (1) **Alexander Lord Elbë**, (2) **Alfred Sidonia** (3) **Fernando De Samara**, who kills himself for her love; steals **Angelica**'s lover, **Amedeus** (**?de Samara**), from her then rejects him; is murdered on **Elmor**'s hillside by **Angelica** and **Douglas**; her body is found by **Lord Eldred**, who muses on her life as brilliant, stormy and brief; later she is lamented by **E.W.** [1, 3, 4, 5, 6, 7, 8, 16, 17, 18, 21, 23, 32, A2]

A., H. either a dark-haired boy or a fair-haired girl (see **S.,A.**(3))

A., J. (and **D.G.C.**) lovers on opposite sides in the war, one royalist the other republican [33]

A., M. imprisoned in a dungeon in Northern College [41]

Alcona, R(osina) loves and is loved by **J(ulius) B(renzaida)** [12] and is the cause of him being in prison, [31]; later, while she is ill, he is murdered; 15 years later she laments his death [36].

Alexander Lord of Elbë (see **Elbë Hall**)

Alexandria a baby left in the snow to die [22]

Alfred (see **Sidonia**)

Alme(i)da, A.G. see **A.G.A.**

Almedore a kingdom in Gaaldine

Amedeus beloved by **Angelica**; seduced by **A.G.A.**; exiled with **Angelica** (**?**nickname for **De Samara**) [21]

Angelica brought up with **A.G.A.**; loves **Amedeus**; seduces **Douglas** into helping murder her rival, **A.G.A.** [21]

Angora a kingdom in **Gondal**; conquered by **Julius Brenzaida** with his crimson standards. [12, A3]

Arthur brother/comrade in arms of **R. Gleneden**, who by his death purchased peace for all [10]

Aspin Castle on shores of **Lake Aspin**, near **Rockden/Beckden** woods; belonging to and haunted by **Lord Alfred Sidonia** [8]

Brenzaida Julius King of **Angora**; became King of **Almedore** in **Gaaldine**; in 1825 is in prison because of **Rosina** [31]; wins victory in battle over **Exina** (green standards) [20]; while in act of becoming joint monarch with **Gerald**, is murdered; buried in **Angora**; has two loves, **Rosina** from whom he is separated when she is ill, [12], and who mourns over his grave 15 years after his death [36], and **Geraldine** who bears him a child with his eyes. [13, 14, 15, A3]

C., D.G. (and **J.A.**) lovers but one a republican, the other a royalist [33]

C., N. (see **Northern College**)

C., R. (and **A.E.**) two very different children [40]

Carlo (see **Tay**)

Claudia exiled but her spirit goes to her own country and her dead monarch [A14]

Colleges two colleges, the **Southern** and the **Northern**, each having a dungeon [17, 31, 32, 41]

Desmond place where **Gleneden** mourns for **Arthur**'s death [10]

Douglas escapes from those who hunt him after he has killed their King; topples a tree on top of them [9]; loves **Angelica** and is implicated by her in **A.G.A.**'s murder [21]

Douglas, M. stands outside **E. R. Gleneden**'s door; reveals he will be reviled for his treachorous deed [35]

E., A.   (see **C., R**) [40]

Eden   in reference to **Ula** [29]; a pleasant place, connected with **de Samara** [17, 32]

Elbë Hall   his noble home, remembered by the dying **Lord Alexander**; beloved by **A.G.A.** [1, 2, 32]

Eldern, Lord   he and his men find **A.G.A.** after she has been murdered [21]

Elderno Lake   trysting place for **de Samara** [17]; later red with blood [12]; connection with the baby **A.A.** [A6]

Elm(?n)or Hill   where **A.G.A.** is murdered [21]

Elnor Lake   where **Lord Alexander Elbë** is murdered [1]

Fernando   (see **de Samara**)

G., E.   (see **E. Gleneden**)

G., M.   prefers the frozen gloom of **Gondal** to **Ula**'s sweet bowers [29]

Gaaldine   large island in the South Pacific divided into six kingdoms: **Alexandria**, **Almedore**, **Elseraden**, **Ula**, **Zelona** (?**Zalona**), **Zedora**; on 12 July 1837 the emperors and empresses leave here to go to Gondal for a coronation; has prison caves where **de Samara** is incarcerated [17]

G., I. (Iernë)   daughter of **I.M.**

Gleneden, E.   pleads with **M.R.** to keep her tryst with him [25]

Gleneden, E. R.   **M. Douglas** tells her that scorn and hatred will blight **Douglas**'s name because of treachery [35]

Gleneden, R.   involved in the battle for **Gondal**, in which his brother, **Arthur**, is killed; owns two dogs, **Tay** and **Carlo** [10]: imprisoned after the murder of the victor, **Julius Brenzaida** [11].

Gobelrin's glen   where Douglas drops a tree on his pursuers [9]

Gondal   remote island in the North Pacific with four kingdoms: **Gondal**, **Angora**, **Alcona**, and **Exina**, its capital **Regina**; 1837 Diary the emperors and empresses of **Gondal** and **Gaaldine** are preparing to leave **Gaaldine** for a coronation in **Gondal** on 12 July; 1841 Diary the Gondalians are in a threatening state, with the princes and princesses at the **Palace of Instruction**; 1845 Diary the Gondal Chronicles, begun three and a half years before, are still not completed. A spare, wild, moorland place. [10, 12, 18, 21, 29]

Julius   (see **Brenzaida**)

Lesley, Lord   dies with **Surry**, whom he loves, when **A.G.A.** is murdered [21]

Lesley Rodric   dies after a battle in 1830 [38]

M., I.   father of **I.G.** [34]

M., Julian   wanders through a dungeon where he finds his childhood friend, **A. G. Rochelle** whom he loves and cares for [42]

Mary   (see **R., M.**)

Northern College   where **A.G.A.** and **M.A.** are imprisoned (see **Colleges**) [32, 42]

Palace of Instruction   where those dedicated to overthrowing the tyrant meet again [19]

R., M. (**Mary**)   **E. Gleneden** reminds her of their promised tryst. [25]

Rochelle A. G.   A fair-haired girl: Julian M.'s playmate: in prison is tended by Julian: describes her 'messenger of Hope' to him. [42]

Rockden (**Beckden**)   near Aspin Castle [8]

Rosina   (see **Alcona**)

S., A. (1)   is told, in 1830, to seek his beloved's grave in the ocean [26]

S., A. (2)   has a brother Gerald: their mother is dead [28]

S., A. (3)   one of two children, the other being **H.A.**, the boy with dark, the girl with fair hair [37]

S., Geraldine   whom **Brenzaida** loves and deserts, she has his child [13, 14, 15]

Samara, Fernando de   sings for **A.G.A.** on **Elderno**'s shores; passionately loves her is put in prison and finally commits suicide because of her [?16, 17, 18]

Sidonia, **Lord Alfred**   of **Aspin Castle**; with blue eyes and fair hair; leaves his ancestral home and a fair-haired daughter for love of **A.G.A.** [4, 5, 6, 8]

Southern College where **Brenzaida** is imprisoned in September 1825 (see **Colleges**) [31]

Surry   lady attendant on **A.G.A.**; loved by **Lord Lesley**; murdered with him when **A.G.A.** is murdered [21]

Tay   (and **Carlo**) **R. Gleneden**'s dogs [10].

Ula   sunny kingdom in **Gaaldine** [29]

U.S.   (the **Unique Society**) shipwrecked on a desert island returning from **Gaul**. [29]

W., E.   laments for **A.G.A.** [23]

Zalona   capital city of a kingdom in **Gaaldine**; besieged and taken; where **Brenzaida** is defeated [20]

Zedora   **Gaaldine** coastal kingdom, governed by a Viceroy; where, in a cave, **Geraldine S.** sings to her baby [15]

The Glasstown Confederacy (references in this book)

Angria   kingdom created for C.'s hero Zamorna, to the east of Glasstown: capital Adrianopolis: has seven provinces, each with its own capital

Glasstown   town built after the original Twelves Town was destroyed: also an area in West Africa where the Young Men settle

Glasstown Confederacy   union of four countries overseen by E.,A.,C. and B. whose combined power was greater than that of any of the individual countries and whose laws and orders had to be obeyed: central government in the Houses of Parliament in Great Glasstown (later Adrianopolis)

Young Men   so-called by B., the original soldiers (the Twelves) who colonize an area in West Africa (see **Glasstown**).

Appendix 2

Spelling and Punctuation

Neither spelling nor punctuation seem to have been Emily Brontë's forte. Where punctuation is concerned, the lines often seem to tumble on to the page, the lack of commas or full-stops giving many a breathless inevitability. The punctuation – or perhaps lack of it – has been retained in the text here.

On the other hand, when a character is speaking, although Emily nearly always carefully enters the quotation marks at the beginning of each line, she often forgets to close them; her spelling, use of capital letters and possessive apostrophes are all erratic. In such circumstances, retaining them would only draw attention to their erratic nature, coming between the reader and the poem. So, where there are no ambiguities, they have been regularized according to modern usage. Her use of capital letters, however, seems to reflect not a grammatical format, but, at times an indifference as to which she uses, at others a tone of voice. She often, for example, uses them to begin words which it seems very likely, she wishes to emphasize. Some letters (f/F for instance) are difficult to differentiate. I have not sought to regularize this except for those that seem merely fortuitous. Where the original is ambiguous or seems to warrant keeping Emily's version, I have done so.

The following is a list of spelling variants:

alter (altar)	forsaw	scearce
aweful	greif	slothfull
bellow (below)	greive	soothe
bravily	hazle (hazel)	souless
breif	hoarsly	stoney
buissy	holyday (text not altered)	streched
carest (caressed)	hopless	their (there)
carless (careless)	inn (in)	tiney (tiny)
caroled (carolled)	intensley	touch
cheerfuly	journy	traitrous
cheif	laureled	tranquility
dazzel	lenghened (lengthened)	truely
devide	lonlier	untill
devine	losing (loosing)	usless (useless)
discry (descry)	majian	vally
dispair	majic	weild
dispondency	matless (mateless)	whach
eternaly	murmer	where (were)
exsistance	mystry	whithered (withered)
extasy	oe'r (o'er)	wisper
fanci	peirced	wistle
faultering	plumy	wonderous
feind	purefyed	wreche (wretch)
firn (fern)	repells	wreched
forelorn	rosey	yeild

Appendix 3

Poems Published in 1846 and 1850

Titles and first lines in the order in which they were printed.

1846

Faith and Despondency	'The winter wind is loud and wild	Gondal 34
Star	Ah! why, because the dazzling sun	EJB 28
The Philosopher	'Enough of thought, philosopher!	EJB 27
Remembrance	Cold in the earth – and the deep snow piled above thee!,	Gondal 36
A Death Scene	O Day! he cannot die	Gondal 32
Song	The linnet in the rocky dells,	Gondal 30
Anticipation	How beautiful the earth is still,	EJB 30
The Prisoner	In the dungeon crypts, idly did I stray, (lines 13–92 of	Gondal 42
	'Silent is the house – all are laid asleep' with an added stanza)	
Hope	Hope was but a timid friend;	EJB 21
A Day-Dream	On a sunny brae, alone I lay	EJB 24
To Imagination	When weary with the long day's care,	EJB 25
How clear she shines! How quietly		EJB 23
Sympathy	There should be no despair for you	EJB 16
Plead for me	Oh, thy bright eyes must answer now,	EJB 26
Self-Interrogation	'The evening passes fast away,	EJB 20
Death	Death! that struck when I was most confiding	EJB 29
Stanzas to –	Well, some may hate, and some may scorn,	EJB 17
Honour's Martyr	The moon is full this winter night;	Gondal 35
Stanzas	I'll not weep that thou art going to leave me,	EJB 10
My Comforter	Well hast thou spoken, and yet, not taught	EJB 22
The Old Stoic	Riches I hold in light esteem;	EJB 8

1850

Stanzas	A little while, a little while	EJB 2
The Bluebell	The Bluebell is the sweetest flower	EJB 4
Stanzas	Loud without the wind was roaring	EJB 1
Shall earth no more inspire thee		EJB 6
The Night Wind	In summer's mellow midnight	EJB 7
Aye – there it is! It wakes to-night		EJB 9
Love and Friendship	Love is like the wild rose-briar	EJB 15
The Elder's Rebuke	'Listen! When your hair, like mine	Gondal 31
The Wanderer from the Fold	How few, of all the hearts that loved	Gondal 23
Warning and Reply	In the earth – the earth – thou shalt be laid	Gondal 27
Last Words	I knew not 'twas so dire a crime	Gondal 14
Loud without the wind was roaring		EJB 1

The Lady to her Guitar For him who struck thy foreign string		Gondal 16
The Two Children Heavy hangs the raindrop		Gondal 40
Child of delight, with sun-bright hair		
The Visionary Silent is the house: all are laid asleep (lines 1–12)		Gondal 42
Encouragment I do not weep; I would not weep		Gondal 28
Stanzas Often rebuked yet always back returning (?E?C – no MS source found: see below)		
No coward soul is mine		EJB 31

Transcriptions by ABN
EJB Notebook nos. 3, 5, 11, 12, 13, 14, 18, 19
Gon Notebook nos. 3, 5, 6, 7, 8, 9, 10, 11, 12, 13, 15, 17, 18, 19, 20, 21, 22, 24, 25, 26, 29, 31, 37, 38, 39, 41

The following stanzas were printed by Charlotte (1850) as by Emily but, while the other 17 poems she printed have been located in Emily's notebooks, the original manuscript for this poem has not been found (see p.13).

'Stanzas'

Often rebuked, yet always back returning
　　To those first feelings that were born with me,
And leaving busy chase of wealth and learning
　　For idle dreams of things which cannot be:

5　To-day, I will seek not the shadowy region;
　　Its unsustaining vastness waxes drear;
And visions rising, legion after legion,
　　Bring the unreal world too strangely near.

I'll walk, but not in old heroic traces,
10　　And not in paths of high morality,
And not among the half-distinguished faces,
　　The clouded forms of long-past history.

I'll walk where my own nature would be leading:
　　It vexes me to choose another guide:
15　Where the grey flocks in ferny glens are feeding;
　　Where the wild wind blows on the mountain side.

What have those lonely mountains worth revealing?
　　More glory and more grief than I can tell:
The earth that wakes *one* human heart to feeling
20　　*Can centre both the worlds of Heaven and Hell.*

Index of First Lines